THOSE DUTCH CATHOLICS

THOSE
DUTCH CATHOLICS

Edited by Michel van der Plas and Henk Suèr

Preface by Desmond Fisher

Jan C. Groot   Henk Suèr

Nico van Hees   Michael van der Plas

Joseph J. Poeisz   Alfred van der Weyer

THE MACMILLAN COMPANY
NEW YORK

© Geoffrey Chapman Ltd, 1967

Translated from the Dutch by Theo Westow

Library of Congress Catalog Card Number: 68–14330

Published in the United States by The Macmillan Company, 1968

Printed and bound in Great Britain

CONTENTS

PREFACE

In the tensions of the post-conciliar period, Holland has become identified with ultra-progressivism. By this is meant that Dutch Roman Catholics are suspected at best of indulging in dangerous ideas and practices which are upsetting the whole Church; at worst of risking a schism. Dutch experiments in liturgy, ecumenism and in the pastoral handling of moral problems have caused reactions ranging from doubt to shock. On the theoretical side, the main areas in which Dutch ideas have been attacked are in the interpretation of the doctrines on the Real Presence in the Eucharist, the virgin birth and the bodily resurrection of Christ. Conservative-minded Catholics in other countries hold up these ideas and practices as a warning of what can happen when the *aggiornamento*, the renewal and reform of the Church, goes too far too fast. Even moderates confess to considerable anxiety about them.

In these areas, as in everything, a little learning is a dangerous thing. It is tempting to erect generalizations on the basis of a few isolated instances. It is easy to exaggerate and distort. Ideas and actions can be misunderstood or only half-understood. Above all, in a Church dominated for four centuries by the attitude that unity means uniformity, developments in a particular socio-religious milieu may be condemned for the insufficient reason that they do not suit the universal Church, at least at this time.

It is essential when evaluating the Dutch scene to know what is happening and why. Theories and practices which to an outsider may appear *outré* or deliberately gimmicky may, on closer acquaintance, be seen to be genuine expressions of a deep and honest search for truth.

This book, therefore, is an attempt to explain why the present developments in Holland came about, what they are and what

7

results they are having. I became convinced of the necessity of
having it written when I heard criticisms of the Dutch Church
from some leading English prelates. I had just come from
Holland where the atmosphere of genuine concern for the future
of the Church and sincere and honest effort to do something
about it was in great contrast with the situation in England. To
hear prelates who had never been to Holland to study developments there condemning them out of hand seemed to me to be not
only grossly unfair but extremely dangerous for the post-
conciliar *aggiornamento*. Contact with many of the outstanding
figures of the Dutch effort to reform and renew the Church,
including some of the authors of the present book, convinced me
that it was possible and vital to clear up some of the
misunderstandings about the Dutch Church which existed in
England and other English-speaking countries. This book is the
result.

Two preliminary points might usefully be made about it. The
first is that the Dutch are what Professor Edward Schillebeeckx,
O.P., of Nijmegen University calls 'a theologizing people'. By
this he means that they see a religious dimension in life to a
greater degree than most other people in the western hemisphere.
They take religion seriously. They revel in theological controversy. This makes for lively speculation and experimentation
even—perhaps especially—at the lay level. This might not be
an unmixed blessing: the proverb has it 'one Dutchman a
theologian; two Dutchmen a sect; three Dutchmen a schism'.
Exaggerated as this is, it gives an idea of the background of
thought in Holland against which this book is written.

The second preliminary point is linked with the first. It is that
the innovations in Holland today are the work of small minority
groups. Notwithstanding the impression one gains from the
international press, the great majority of Dutch Catholics are
comparatively traditional in their religious attitudes. Where they
differ from conservative-minded Catholics in other countries,
particularly in the English-speaking ones, is that they are not
simultaneously illiberal. With some few exceptions, they believe
that the minority of progressives should have freedom to put
forward their points of view and to conduct their experiments.

Since tolerance of different opinions on matters which are not essential to the faith could be regarded as the chief mark of progressive thinking among Catholics today, it is probably fair to say that there are few real conservatives in Holland: it is a matter of different degrees of progressivism.

I hope this book will leave the reader with three main conclusions. The first is that the Dutch Catholic progressives are proving that unity in the Church does not demand uniformity. There is no tendency to schism in Holland, despite what prejudiced observers in other countries may say, though there is a deep suspicion of the Roman Curia and a widespread disappointment with Pope Paul's failure to push the *aggiornamento* ahead faster. But the need for unity within the universal Church, as represented in the person of the pope, is recognized.

But within this unity—and this is the second and most important conclusion the reader of this book should draw—there is room for pluriformity. What the Dutch are doing is to revive the idea of the local Church which was so prominent in apostolic times, as witness the epistles to the Church in Ephesus, the Church which is at Corinth, and so on. The Dutch see the local Church as the embodiment in a particular place of the universal Church. As Cardinal Bernard Alfrink of Utrecht told the opening session of the European Bishops' Symposium at Noordwijkerhout, Holland, on 10 July 1967: 'The local Church is not merely part of a larger whole. Further, it is in the local Churches that the one mystery of the Church of Christ is incarnated in a concrete way in our history. Without the reality of the local Churches the one Church of Christ is not to be found on earth.' This idea of pluriformity in unity has been lost sight of in the post-Tridentine defensive era of Catholicism. The Dutch are bringing it back.

Finally, the Dutch progressives—and most of the contributors to this book fall into that category—recognize that what they are trying involves danger. But they believe that the greater danger lies in doing nothing. They see disturbance and anxiety as a comparatively small price to pay for the deeper insights the new thinking may bring and the possibility they hold out of renewing and reforming the Church.

They believe that the traditional practices and doctrines of the

Church must be thoroughly re-examined, not in order to sup-
plant them but in order to develop them more fully. Otherwise,
they say, the Church is failing in her central task of being 'the
light of the world', as the Vatican Council's Constitution on
the Church presents her.

To put it in short, the Dutch believe with Karl Rahner that the
Church must change with this changing world if it is to remain
the same.

INTRODUCTION

Michel van der Plas and Henk Suèr

Dutch Catholicism is in the news. It is reported in a large number of foreign newspapers and magazines, but there has rarely been an attempt at presenting a coherent picture of the true situation and its complex background. Even the most intelligent observers within the Dutch community itself admit that their views are no more than partial views. Reports are often coloured because reporters are sent to find out about a particular incident or person, or because the situation is approached with a certain prejudice, not infrequently inspired by high officials in the Church.

This book hopes to be a guide through the labyrinth which Dutch Catholicism seems to be not only for the bewildered foreigner but, to be honest, for most of the Dutch themselves. In this book it will be pointed out that the Dutch are not unduly worried about all this publicity, even if it is unpleasant: they are stubborn by nature and will no doubt go on thinking, practising and experimenting in their own way, at least for the time being.

Nevertheless, some of us believe that to allow a false image to build up outside might lead to a dangerous isolation of the Dutch Church, which would neither benefit the Dutch nor the Church universal. Talk about a 'Dutch schism' in the making is particularly offensive. We think, rather, that Dutch Catholics have a contribution to make to Catholicism at large. The attempt to isolate the Dutch and the persistent, uncalled-for and unjustifiable condemnation of the Dutch by a few vocal, badly-informed critics may well bring about a dangerous misunderstanding, and this would have pernicious consequences for the renewal of the Church at large.

In this book we have tried to present an objective picture of the Catholic community in Holland. We were not interested in

11

apologetics but simply in providing, as Dutch Catholic journalists, the basic, honest information which will allow the reader to
reach his own conclusions.

The position of Dutch Catholics in the world Church today
sometimes recalls the position of the last non-Italian pope in
Church history up till now, the Dutch Adrian VI (1522-23).
When Friedrich von Schiller mentioned him in his essay 'On
naïve and sentimental poetry' (*Ueber naïve und sentimentalische
Dichtung*), he rightly described this pope as 'a truly naïve
character at one of the most critical moments' of the Church,
when, for instance, he confessed to faults which the Church,
under heavy attack from the Reformers, had so far neglected to
face up to in a realistic way. His predecessors had stuck to the
principle of never yielding an inch on any front.

'Adrian VI,' wrote Schiller, 'possessed the character of his
compatriots, accustomed to grasp nettles firmly and boldly. He
could be proud of the integrity of his former position. . . . He was
far too sensible a man to deny in public what he had been forced
to admit in private.' And Schiller added, 'One can easily
understand how the Roman clergy looked upon this kind of
naïvety.'

Rightly or wrongly, the Dutch Catholics continue to speak and
act 'naïvely' in a Church and a world, which today, as then, are
beset by many crises.

1. WHAT IS GOING ON IN THE DUTCH CHURCH?

MICHEL VAN DER PLAS

The interested foreigner who wants to see for himself what truth there is in those alarming stories about Catholics in Holland will find it difficult to know where to look for it. If, on a Sunday morning, he enters an ordinary parish church, he will see something that may appeal to him, but nothing shocking. He will find it difficult to find a seat in the crowded pews. He will notice that there are as many men as women, and a vast number of children and young people.

The behaviour of these people is disciplined and respectful. With their 'missal-leaflet' for the day in their hands they kneel, sit or stand all together. Prayers and responses proceed in orderly fashion and all speak up. The visitor will not understand the sermon, but if he cares to ask someone what it was about he will find that there was no theological attack on heaven nor any revolutionary morality. It will not escape him that the collection plates are well filled, and when the moment of communion arrives he will see impressively long queues of faithful move towards the communion rails.

This visit to the church will hardly have knocked him sideways. His first impression of Dutch Catholics will be that they are a manageable, sober and devout church-going people. Perhaps he will have noticed the stiff backs and the solemn faces and have the impression that the average Dutchman's faith does not exactly express itself exuberantly. But he will come to see that these are a serious people who face their responsibilities, take their duties seriously, disapprove of nonchalance, keep their word scrupulously and are rather too embarrassed to show the warmth of their heart. The Dutch are direct and persevering in their quest for Christ's new creation. Their great historian Huizinga wrote this about his people: 'It is and remains one of the most

13

precious features of the Dutch spirit that it is capable of receiving
influences of many kinds and of assimilating the views of other
nations without ever losing the essence of its own nationality.'

Would this superficial first impression of Dutch Catholics be
false? An unceasing stream of publications, friendly and hostile,
depicts them as rebels of the universal Church, dangerously
skimming the edge of the abyss of heresy. Is the spectacle of
devout church-goers no more than a façade behind which there is
a vast process of de-Christianization going on? Newspapers
report extraordinary movements and experiments in the
Church of Holland. Some of these matters seem so unortho-
dox that eyebrows are raised, not only in other provinces of
the Church but even more at the centre, in Rome. Where does
the truth lie?

In actual fact, in the recent past a number of unusual things
have been written about, preached and experimented with. It *is*
true that there *are* a number of parish churches where the bishop
has allowed an unusual liturgical service, where the faithful
receive the host in their hands, and where layfolk are allowed to
share the chalice which contains the wine that is the blood of
Christ. There *are* services where young people are allowed to oust
the organ with their electric guitars and drums when they sing
negro spirituals and perform their 'beat' masses. There *are* parish
priests, perhaps two or three, who try to brighten the interior of
their church with a large aviary or an illuminated aquarium. It is
true that there has been a kind of iconoclasm: innumerable
plaster saints have been hauled down from their pedestals. And it
is quite certainly *possible* that a preacher occasionally and
suddenly comes out with a bit of exegesis which would make the
theologian gape with astonishment.

One might prolong this enumeration of more or less 'shocking'
developments *ad libitum*. There is *some* truth in the many odd
bits of news that occasionally cause a sensation abroad through
the foreign press. The facts are often much less sensational than
the manner in which they are publicized. Thus, to give an
example, it is not particularly sensational that in a country like
Holland, which has about 8,000 priests, some sixty have

abandoned their calling. But what makes the case of Holland different is that there the subject is openly discussed. It was world news when the late Bishop Bekkers said publicly from a pulpit in Eindhoven that both the parish priest and one of the curates had decided to leave the priesthood. Such a gesture by a bishop is highly appreciated in Holland because the Dutch detest secrecy. On the other hand, this same attitude has occasionally led an individual laicized priest to announce his marriage in an unusually royal manner. In some recent publications some ex-priests have wanted to justify their action, and in doing so have somewhat lavishly criticized their seminary training, the lack of communication between bishops and clergy, the lack of democracy in the Church and all kinds of dishonesty and hypocrisy. Such books are published by Catholic publishers and nobody blames them for it.

Criticism does go on, almost gleefully. Here is a random sample, a short 'Letter to the Editor' of the Catholic daily *De Tijd,* which incidentally reveals something of the Dutch attitude to the Roman Curia:

'For years you have reported, with the regularity of the lunar cycle, that, according to rumours, the Roman Curia will be reformed before long. Could you possibly tell me to what kind of literary or journalistic genre this report belongs? Would it not be a good idea to give it regular space on the humour page every Saturday?'

There have been inquiries in Holland as to whether celibacy must be a necessary condition of the priesthood. More than one-third of the priests said no. Soon minor seminaries in their present form will practically disappear. Nor will it be long before students for the priesthood will follow lectures in the same classroom as girls of their own age. Major seminaries are also disappearing. A number of them will merge because of lack of students; the Church authorities, moreover, think it healthier for their students to follow lectures at the theological faculties of the existing (mainly non-Catholic) universities, although most will probably enrol at the Catholic University of Nijmegen.

The changes lose much of their sensational value when seen in the overall context of the renewal which Vatican II set going in

Holland. Yet the expression given to this renewal leads one to think that much more is stirring than appears. Catholic dailies, weeklies and monthlies with large circulations regularly print articles that deal with speculative theology so that a large public can get acquainted with fresh, new (and occasionally perhaps somewhat foolhardy) theories about transubstantiation, Mary's virginity, the veneration of saints, evolution, the resurrection, and so on.

A number of things happen today that would have been unthinkable ten or even five years ago. At that time many Catholics would certainly have been surprised to hear some well-known priests say, immediately before the general elections, that in their opinion the best way of using one's vote is to vote for the left-wing, pacifist, socialist party. Today people agree that these priests have a right to a personal opinion, and if people argue with them it will only be at the level of politics. Next, a priest's housekeeper writes in the official weekly of the diocese of Breda that most priests are not fit to marry anyway. ('They do not even notice that somebody looks after them, let alone that it is a woman who does it all.') This, of course, unleashes a veritable storm of amusing protests from numerous presbyteries—the clergy are quite convinced that they would make excellent husbands. Even before the controversy has calmed down, after being duly exploited by the comedians of the press, a new topic occupies the platform. A Catholic priest, N. van Hees, editor of the socialist paper *Het Vrije Volk*, is also appointed editor of the official publication of the Dutch Society for Sex Reform (which Catholics used to call the Neo-Malthusian Society). The name of this publication is *Responsible Parenthood* which the wits were not slow to change into 'Irresponsible Priesthood'. But there is no quarrel. On the contrary, the same day the papers announce that the Society for Sex Reform has appointed a new Director who is also a Catholic.

Within one year three bishops died in Holland. Three times a diocesan chapter decided to draft its list of nominations democratically and asked the people of the diocese to suggest names of their own choice. It is hardly possible any longer to think of

a bishop's appointment without the voice of the faithful being
heard in the chapter.

It is also true that an increasing number of young Catholic
women use 'the pill' since they either do not want to wait for a
papal statement or find it irrelevant. More people also advocate
the secularizing of Catholic organizations, and this, of course,
opens up the issue of Catholic education. An inquiry showed
that a surprising number of lay people who take part in discussion
groups think it quite possible to lead a genuine Christian life outside the Church.

All this *does* happen, and one could give many other examples
of the 'advanced' mentality of some Dutch Catholics. It is therefore hardly surprising that there are also faithful of a more traditional turn of mind who are 'shocked' by all this.

The average Catholic feels deeply involved in all these
developments. He is profoundly interested in his religion; this has
always been more or less the case, but now more than ever.
Someone once said that one Dutchman is a religion, two
Dutchmen found a Church, and three will produce a schism. In
the past, religious disputes unfortunately created rifts, particularly among Protestant Christians, but the very continuity of
these disputes kept interest in religion alive. One can say many
things about Dutch Christians but not that they are only half
awake. And if, at the moment, this lively interest is accompanied
by a certain amount of unrest, this unrest is the living sign of the
basic conviction that we live in an age when to be or not to be a
Christian is a decisive issue. This means for some the beginning
of the end, for others it means that Christianity at long last begins
to shed the marks of its infancy.

One cannot help wondering occasionally whether the criticism
meted out to the Catholics of Holland by people from outside
does not spring from an ill-repressed jealousy. It is possible to be
jealous of the intense social vitality and reactions of the simple
faithful. This may sound a little smug, but one can, in all fairness,
maintain that certain circles in Rome were frightened by the realization that there really were Catholics who took Vatican II
seriously and were determined to pursue its conclusions and
put them into practice.

On reading this brief sketch one may wonder whether these or similar things do not happen anywhere else, and of course they do. Holland represents no more than one percent of the universal Church and much is going on in other countries. The only difference seems to be that in Holland everything is happening at once. The process is complicated by the fact that everywhere, at the social level, the 'establishment' is subject to ruthless questioning.

In so far as Church matters are concerned it is typical of Holland that everything is immediately made public, while elsewhere there is an inclination to suffer in silence. We admit that the Dutch act in a way which is neither always perfectly controlled nor very clever. They, too, occasionally lose a sense of the relativity of their problems. But by bringing them into the open they arrive at a relief of tension, they foster communication and so there grows, with the recognition of each other's difficulties, a sense of Christian 'togetherness' (as the Americans would call it), which in any case eliminates an ostrich policy. For it is nothing but ostrich policy to suppress the publication of what is going on among fellow-Christians – and nothing is more frustrating.

Not everything that happens in the Dutch Church is always reported fairly and objectively in other countries. Cardinal Alfrink, who daily receives letters from all over the world from people who are indignant or shocked, has frequently murmured that he is not sure whether this international interest in his rather small province of the Church is a source of joy. Sometimes the Dutch are accused of getting swept off their feet by fashions and, as an example of this, people point to the tens of thousands of copies of *Honest to God* that have been sold in Holland. But should someone simply set out to be 'with it', the reaction of his compatriots will soon tell him so. The minorities that do not agree with the renewal in certain fields, at any rate make their rejection plain in a way which leaves no doubt. And this leads to new adjustments. But there have also been recent discussions which were not exactly an example of Christian tolerance. A number of those who are upset are vocal and persistent, and sometimes get their way. It is probably due to them that with the successful introduction of the vernacular the old Latin Mass did not disappear and so the Catholic can follow his Sunday liturgy in the traditional Latin, if he so wishes.

One group of 'traditionalists', who have their own magazine *Confrontatie*, at the end of 1966 criticized the new Catechism for the Dutch Province. This Catechism was commissioned by the Dutch hierarchy who have assumed responsibility for it. But in their indignation the group went behind the backs of the bishops and sent a petition to the Pope to have it either withdrawn or basically revised. This way of doing things was considered rather 'bad form'; it smacked of those peculiarly secret and underhand methods that had been used in the past. One paper managed to secure the text of the petition and to make it public even before it reached the Pope. This incident has somewhat spoiled the atmosphere and has won little sympathy for the *Confrontatie* group. Sometimes the conservatives accuse the progressives of deliberately 'occupying' the main media for Catholic publicity. The average layman, they say, should be able to listen also to the more traditional arguments.

The bishops are in all this faced with the difficult task of guiding their faithful who insist partly on clear directives and partly on as much freedom as possible to think out the new situation and to experiment. The difficulty is further increased by their profound loyalty to the Pope and the universal Church on the one hand, and their keen appreciation of the right, and even the duty, to pluriformity which implies considerable freedom of action.

Yet, in spite of the tensions and difficulties the situation is a source of joy. Foreign observers, and there are plenty of them, do not always see this. And if they are Church leaders one can detect, in their statements, their worry about the spread of Dutch ideas and experiments in their own dioceses or provinces. An example is the reaction of Cardinal Ottaviani, secretary to the Congregation of Doctrine, to the Dutch Pastoral Council: he declared recently and in public that this Council does not deserve the name. Immersed as he is in Canon Law, he can find there no legal precedent for the kind of internal deliberations that are taking place in the Church of Holland. Another example is

the reaction of the French Cardinal-Archbishop of Bourges to a
report in *Paris Match* on the liturgical experiments in Holland:
about the 'new Mass' he said, 'We have here, without any doubt,
quite exceptional facts and, in so far as the more shocking photos
are concerned, they show not real Catholics, but rather a sect
which in one and the same celebration unites Christians of
various confessions.'

Reactions from Rome particularly upset Dutch Catholics. It
is constantly suggested in the foreign press that every time the
Pope is worried he has the Dutch situation in mind. The encyclical
Mysterium Fidei was said to be aimed directly at some unusual
theological theories about the Eucharist, mooted in Dutch
publications.

But to set against these reactions there are others. In the United
States a striking number of Catholics follow what is going on in
Holland and do things, usually of a practical nature, which seem
to correspond directly to the needs which the Dutch have felt in
their own country. The authoritative French paper *Le Monde*
praises Dutch Catholicism for its vitality, 'a source of astonishment for the foreigner', and says that the new Catechism is 'very
significant, a renewal of the ways in which the faith is put across,
closer to the Bible than to the usual theological formulae'. In the
New York Times Clyde Farnsworth wrote, 'The Dutch lead the
way in the movement inaugurated by Pope John to bring new life
to the Catholic Church and to give the faith a new significance in
this modern world.' According to this author the Dutch Catholics
have acted far more swiftly and have made more progress than
any others in Pope John's *aggiornamento*. In *Le Figaro* René
Laurentin wrote,

'In any case, the climate in the Dutch Catholic Church is
dynamic and active; nobody needs to pity the Dutch. What the
Dutch are doing often rouses admiration or violent reaction,
but never pity. Superficially it looks as if they want to change
everything, dogma, the Mass, and traditional morality. But
looked at closely they are mainly concerned with the question
of how far the dogmas and the biblical data are to be correctly
presented, so as to show through the myths of an out-of-date
mentality.'

Recently the new pro-prefect of the Congregation of Studies in Rome, Monsignor Garonne, said that in any case one should not judge the Dutch too quickly and superficially: their experiments deserve serious attention. He did not, of course, go so far as Paul Johnson, chief editor of the *New Statesman,* who wrote, 'I should like to see the Vatican abolished and head-quarters moved to a country (Holland, for instance) where there is a better climate for discussion.'

In general one may say that reactions abroad do not trouble the average Dutch Catholic very much—he quietly goes his own way. Some will see the writing on the wall in the fact that this same average Catholic takes reactions from Rome more or less for granted. But it has happened too often in the past that Rome was badly informed about burning issues in distant provinces of the Church. Too often, too, the Curia has been *a priori* opposed to any new movements without bothering to examine them thoroughly on their merits. Moreover, Vatican II showed re-peatedly that opinions which ran counter to those of well-known curial prelates often proved to be perfectly tenable and were at a later stage fully approved by a large majority of bishops. So one cannot blame the Dutch Catholic for taking Roman reactions with a pinch of salt.

At the moment, however, many Dutch Catholics are beginning to feel the need to consolidate what has so far been achieved rather than to prolong the unrest in theology and morality. There is a widespread desire for a period of rest and for 'thinking things over'. The *avant-garde* keeps on pegging out more and more unknown territory, and not every Catholic who reads about it in his paper is ready or even willing to follow. It would appear that the present Pastoral Council is precisely inspired by the desire to 'take stock'—at any rate this is how many Catholics look on this unique event.

It is, as always in such questions, extremely difficult, if not impossible, to generalize about *the* Dutch Catholic. The majority will certainly not identify themselves with some of the extreme progressives. It might therefore be wiser at this stage to note down just a few tendencies which may be considered as generally valid.

The first of these general tendencies is a deeply felt need to enrich the old truths of the faith, not only in the light of what the various sciences have established, but also in view of the urgent demands of a society that is undergoing a radical change, and where the Christian can no longer allow himself to live in a ghetto. He is forced to be fully present, active and ready to serve. This is reinforced in the case of the Dutchman by the keen interest in theological problems, with a strongly practical slant, which he has inherited from his ancestors.

The second tendency is to leave as much freedom as they need to those who are honest and realistic in their pursuit of truth. This means that all will uphold the right of freedom of serious investigation, and will instinctively resent actions that limit this freedom, dismiss professors and teachers, or try to prevent or forbid publication of ideas.

Closely linked with this is a deep-seated desire to make the Church democratic. One sometimes wonders how the Church, with its present hierarchical structure, can ever become a democracy. However, there is a wish that at least the principles of democracy should be applied as broadly as possible. This is illustrated by the present Pastoral Council. What strikes one here is the consultation of the ordinary faithful by means of discussion groups and the 'post-box' arrangement which encourages every Catholic to put his criticisms, suggestions and wishes in writing, in the sure knowledge that he will be listened to.

The next general tendency has been concisely described by an English journalist: 'The Dutch Catholic Church believes in starting from the other end. It believes in starting from Holland and not from Rome. It believes in starting from the individual human being and not from abstract moral laws.' With this is connected the popularity of the idea of pluriformity in Holland. This is not merely a matter of pluriformity in matters of liturgy, or training for the priesthood or ecumenical activity, but, and perhaps mainly, of recognizing the principle of plurality in the field of theology. As Fr R. Adolfs, O.S.A., has put it,

'What we want is to be allowed to theologize freely in our own way. The Dutch Catholic Church is a Church in dialogue, not only with Protestants but also with humanists and atheists. In such a situation we cannot simply stick rigidly to a traditional Roman way of doing theology. There is a whole movement of new theological reflection about the person of Jesus Christ, for example, and this must be allowed to come into the open.'

The average Dutch Catholic wonders how, in the present structure of the Church, Rome will understand and tolerate this pluriformity. The local Church is indeed *the* Church in our country. The Dutch in no way expect other Churches to be the same as theirs, but they do expect that developments similar to theirs will take place elsewhere in the universal Church— developments adjusted to the character and culture of the people concerned.

A number of Dutch commentators were more than usually struck at the Council by Cardinal Lercaro's intervention on 4 November 1964 on the question of cultural values within the Church. One of them called it the most progressive statement of the whole Council. The Cardinal asked whether it was not high time to examine 'what essential changes must be made in the whole cultural order which prevails within the Church, and what changes were clearly demanded at this moment for the special cultural situation of our days'. The Church ought to admit her cultural poverty; what was considered a rich culture in the past, he said, no longer appealed to the modern mind:

'If necessary, the Church should resolutely put aside those cultural achievements of the past or at least not put her trust in them. She should not boast too much of them and only use them cautiously. For they do not always put the light of the gospel on the candlestick, but frequently hide it under a bushel. They frequently prevent the Church from making modern culture and the treasures of old non-Christian cultures her own. . . . The Church has always denied that she identified herself or her doctrine with one system or another, one particular philosophy or theology. Up till now, however, this distinction was more *de jure* than *de facto*. The moment has come when the Church and her essential message must be *de facto*, every day more and more detached from a cultural code or *"organon"*, the permanent and universal character of which is

still taken too seriously by many people, moved as they are by a
spirit of conservatism and smugness.'

The Cardinal then turned to 'the re-discovery of Holy
Scripture, biblical language and mentality', and to the use of a
different type of language for the dialogue both within the
Church and in its communication with the world. 'If the official
language in which we are still forced to think is, in spite of a
glorious past, dead today and no longer universal, i.e. no longer
capable of expressing the new ideas which are everywhere in use',
how can the Church fulfil her mission for men and women of this
age?

I believe that Dutch Catholics, partly consciously, partly
subconsciously, are convinced of the need for this process of
'cleaning up', as proposed by Cardinal Lercaro. The enrichment
of the truths of the faith, still proclaimed in a rigid and dull way,
through a new attitude and new forms of expression is felt as a
necessity which has to be met, even if this entails a temporary
'cold war' situation with the curial mentality of Rome.

A minority will be inclined to draw more radical consequences
from this necessity than the great majority can swallow. Many
want a gradual process, although it is always surprising to see
time and again how quickly the average Catholic in Holland can
assimilate new ideas, as long as he sees their inevitability. A
typical example of this is the discussion about celibacy. Within
a very few years a majority has come to see clearly that our age
seems to demand the disentanglement of the priesthood from
celibacy as an exclusive condition. Another example is the doubt
about the applicability of that famous adage—*Roma locuta, causa
finita*—rather too lavishly bandied about in the past. More than
ever before, even compared with quite recent times, the average
Catholic in Holland looks upon his bishop as the one to be
listened to first; the bishops are now regarded as pastors with
whom a genuine and realistic dialogue is possible. The bishops
have become more human and are no longer the vague 'princes of
the Church' on their thrones in papal Rome, not even in their own
mind; the people have discovered with increasing force that they
share with their bishops in a common vulnerability.

This new development has found expression in a series of short poems by the poet Huub Oosterhuis, of which I would like to quote two. The first, 'The Bishop', seems to be inspired by the deeply lamented late Bishop Bekkers:

> O what fun to be a bishop
> To help between acts the milkman
> At the door, while your fellowmen
> Are shaking their heads.
>
> To share in public activity
> With your consecrated hands.
> In countless eyes you are reflected
> First, then multiplied.
>
> You eat the bread of the poor
> Albeit still with a silver spoon.
> Then, one morning, there appears
> The detective from Rome.

The second is entitled 'Cardinal':

> Now let us pray
> In our mother tongue
> For that man most stared at
> In our midst, the Cardinal.
>
> For, dear God, this is worrying us,
> That somehow he is neither more
> Nor less than an elderly, pleasant,
> And very lonely gentleman.
>
> And, take it from me, it is not easy
> To drop in casually and meet
> All the others, in all that red,
> And to beg for some bread.

It would be silly to deny that there is a crisis in the Catholic Church in Holland. As has been proved by careful analysis and assessment, the heart of this crisis does not lie in the mass of the faithful but in the clergy (particularly the post-war clergy) and the young intellectuals. It would be equally silly to deny that this crisis has created a more or less general unrest among the faithful.

But it must be firmly stated at the same time that more and more
Catholics live in peace with this unrest. I mean that they are
learning that a faith without uncertainties is hardly thinkable, and
even hardly desirable for a sound inner life. The average Dutch
Catholic is in the situation of Gertrude Stein on her deathbed:
she asked, 'What is the answer?' When no answer came, she
laughed and said, 'In that case, what is the question?'

Prof. Schillebeeckx put it as follows:

'There is a general unrest or lack of ease which is common to
man whenever he has to shed old habits, if this shedding is not
prompted by a personal, existentially felt need but is imposed
by the society in which he lives, [Gertrude Stein does indeed ask
first for the answer, but when it is not forthcoming she is
forced to ask what the real question is] as is now happening in
the life of the liturgy because of the Council. ... For many this
means inevitably something like flaying oneself of one's own
skin. This is not a plea for half-baked renewals that would
leave *everybody* dissatisfied, rather it is a plea that there be a
genuine understanding of the sacrifices which are asked of some
so that the Church may live. The fact is that the self-emptying
required of others is not given sufficient public recognition, and
one of the many factors creating the unrest in Holland is this
kind of public tug-of-war that is going on. It is often forgotten
in this connection that what is old suddenly acquires a new
glamour when it is cast aside, while on the other hand one ought
to remember that any order, new or old, is bound to have advantages and disadvantages. As a result people who surround
the old order with glamour—rather late in the day—are inclined
to see only the (real) disadvantages of the new.

'... Sometimes one is under the impression that at present in
Holland "principles" and (old or new) "ideology", whether in
religion or in politics, are more important than the *people*
themselves. In any case, in so far as I am concerned personally,
life in Holland forces me to take myself seriously, a state which
I would not have reached outside Holland or simply by
myself.'

The crisis, according to him, is nothing less but also nothing
more than a *crisis of growth*.

The Dutch are aware that what is happening in Holland is not necessarily *the* crisis of growth which the whole Church must go through in exactly the same way. Many doubt whether it is desirable that more and more new difficulties accumulate round more and more traditional data of the faith, or about the real contents of theories launched by people who are not always experts, or whether the many new ideas suggested contain those that are most important for the development and practice of the faith in our age. Others wonder whether there is still room for a normal devout life that has some continuity with tradition if the great facts of salvation are always accompanied by question-marks and so rarely with exclamation-marks. Is it, for instance, necessary, they ask, for a priest who gives the epilogue on television on great feastdays to send us to bed with theological worries instead of a little word of devout encouragement?

Even the more radical supporters of the renewal have started recently to doubt, quietly or out loud, whether we in Holland are on the right track about absolutely everything. It is realized that there is a good deal of truth in the criticism that Dutch Catholics are too much inclined to devalue symbols too radically. As an English observer, John Wilkins, put it,

'They do not allow symbols simply to speak for themselves. They always ask, "What is it *for*? What does it *mean* in terms of today?" They are not good at seeing how through symbols that you do know you grasp the things that you don't know. I found that "romance" is a dirty word in Holland. There seems to be a widespread loss of any sense of the Church as a "mother"; or again they have described Christ's action in the Eucharist as something like a hostess handing out cups of tea to her guests, or like a father giving his children chocolate before they go to bed. There is a banality about that which is frightening, although at least it has given rise to one of the best Protestant quips: "Formerly everything remained the same, except for the bread and wine, which changed. Now everything changes except for the bread and wine which stay the same." Such criticisms are in place because the Dutch Catholic progressives would be the first to acknowledge that their own insights are only partial. All they are asking is to be allowed to work things out in their own way.'

This seems fair. One might add that Holland has never been particularly rich in mystical experiences and writings.

Yet one can be certain that this crisis of growth with its critical aspects is generally felt as necessary and, in the wider context of the universal Church, is seen as significant in the sense that other provinces of the Church will, in some way or other, draw benefit from the experiences that Holland is going through. In all this the Dutch Catholic has reckoned with the risk he runs of himself having to suffer most from this crisis of growth.

Anyway, one thing is certain in all its simplicity and that is that to the question, 'What is going on in Holland?' he may at least confidently answer—'We are alive.'

2. THE DUTCH CHURCH YESTERDAY

HENK SUÈR

In the past Dutch Catholics played but a limited part within the Church as a whole. The one and only Dutch pope, Adrian VI, occupied the see of Peter only for one year, with little opportunity to put his own ideas into practice. There are few canonized Dutch saints. On the whole the Dutch do not consider themselves particularly gifted in the field of holiness, and though they honour the names of great social pioneers, they are not in a hurry to have them officially canonized; such efforts have never had any massive support. Thomas à Kempis' *Imitation of Christ* spread throughout Western Europe at the end of the Middle Ages but this success is the more marked in view of the general lack of influential thinkers and theologians among the Christians of the Rhine delta. Fortunately, there was Erasmus who with his *Praise of Folly* and his cosmopolitan career linked the Low Countries with the great European event of the Renaissance. Although there has been a general inclination to look on his humanism as a peculiar Christian deviation, Dutch Catholics were no more ashamed of his habits and his vision than they were of the paintings and engravings of biblical themes by Rembrandt, who was not a particularly assiduous church-goer.

However, whatever the small Dutch Church may have contributed in the past is not all of merely local interest. Rome's pride has been flattered for a long time by the devotion that flowed to it from this misty corner of Northern Europe in the shape of financial contributions and manpower for the curial offices and the army. Since the turn of this century the Dutch Church has become particularly important for its exceptionally high number of missionaries. Literally tens of thousands of priests, Brothers and Sisters have left Holland to preach the gospel and take care of the needy all over the world. In this field only the Irish can compete with the Dutch.

Since much of what is happening now in the Dutch Church can only be understood in the light of the past, it might be useful to select a few historical events and circumstances for further elucidation.[1] On this basis I put a number of questions to a group of historians of the Theological Faculty of Nijmegen University. I have kept this form of question and answer in order to make plain that this chapter is not so much a careful piece of historical writing as a somewhat hasty glimpse at matters that are of interest for the present situation and therefore worth mentioning.

Dutch Catholicism is going through a crisis. Some take this as a disease, others as a transition, but all agree that something far-reaching is happening. Are there any periods in the past with which we may compare the present situation?

Seen in the right light, we are passing through the same kind of radical change as took place at the beginning of the Reformation. The attitudes of many people today towards the faith are very different from those of ten years ago although there has been no break with the past. It is only now that we can begin to understand the swift success of the Reformation. A priest would celebrate a Catholic Mass in the morning while he led a Reformed service in the evening. There are also, of course, vast differences between the changes of that period and those of today. For Holland, the motivation of the Reformation was political as well as doctrinal; it became a patriotic movement, opposed to the power of Spain which regarded Catholicism as the 'established' religion and introduced the inquisition. Holland became a Calvinist country and the Roman churches were handed over to the Protestants, and purified from foreign elements.

[1] The Dutchman himself can consult L. Rogier's and N. de Rooy's very popular work, *In Vrijheid Herboren* (Born again in Freedom), for the more recent developments. Certain details have been added to this by G. Abbink, a seminary professor, in an article that appeared in *Tijdschrift voor Theologie*, 1965, n.3.

What was the result of this setback for Dutch Catholics?

They took it as a disaster and an infringement of their rights. They found no support anywhere and became liable to persecution. To assist at Mass they met in secret, in the homes of merchants or farmers' barns. Socially, a Catholic had no standing, and this held particularly for priests, in contrast to their colleagues in Germany, Austria, France and Italy where bishops and monasteries were wealthy, privileged and politically influential. In those countries Catholicism expressed itself in extravagantly celebrated liturgical services in baroque churches, where the ordinary people had to maintain a respectful distance from the altar and the priests. This distance did not exist in Holland. There the Church could only stay alive through a sincere and firm faith and an unwavering loyalty on the part of Catholics. The Dutch priest, whose possessions were frequently confiscated, could only choose his vocation out of sheer generosity. He was close to the people and had their confidence.

Was this Catholic minority as small as it looked?

In fact, this minority has always been greater than was realized. This clandestine Catholicism lived in such a modest and withdrawn atmosphere that practically no one had any idea of the actual numbers. Yet it constituted the second largest group of the population, always varying between approximately thirty-five and forty percent. Most of the Catholics lived in the South which had few political and economic links with the dominant West. The South accepted this isolation without great difficulty. Here and there rigid attitudes did develop, as is often the case with minorities. There was no tendency to knuckle under to puritan Calvinism, and the hostility between the two was quite open.

Were there any advantages in this isolation?

The Catholic population was saved the trouble which beset such countries as France, Austria and Germany, with such disastrous consequences. In those countries there was a fierce struggle about an open or closed Catholicism and about the

Church's freedom in a free state, a struggle which caused deep
rifts. Theologians were in conflict with the hierarchy about their
academic freedom. This sometimes went to such lengths that
many left the Church. None of this took place in Holland where
oppression made Catholics look to unity for salvation, so that
Rome became the symbol of unity. It was difficult to get into
trouble with Rome on administrative matters since, during the
period that Dutch Catholicism was governed directly from Rome
through a nuncio, the nuncio was never allowed to enter his
territory.

The revolutionary movements that shook Europe in 1789 and
1848 told against the Church because the Church had identified itself too completely with the wealthy and privileged
classes. There were sharp condemnations of the ideals of freedom
which the revolutionaries upheld. This negative attitude led to
apostasy and anti-clericalism in several countries. But even this
development hardly caused a ripple in Dutch Catholicism. The
archpriests, who may be compared to bishops, were no grandees,
no great lords, as elsewhere. Dutch Catholics passed through the
first half of the nineteenth century in a sheltered and undisturbed
atmosphere. They were still the clandestine group of the earlier
period, of no significance in public life, usually engaged in farming
or small businesses. They were excluded from government and
judicial offices and took no, or very little, part in the growing
industralization of the country.

But gradually something must have come to life in this group?

Among the more well-to-do of small Catholic towns there arose
a demand for social emancipation. The ideas of the French revo-
lution which had spread into Holland endowed Catholics, along
with the rest of the country, with constitutional liberty and
equality. Dutch liberals sought the political support of the
Catholic population, which was not numerically insignificant.
These liberals were prepared to co-operate towards a restoration
of the Catholic hierarchy, which some Catholics had been demanding in Rome. To the Church at large, Holland was still a
mission country.

Why was Rome easily persuaded to agree to restoration?

In 1853, three years after the restoration of the hierarchy in England, it was Holland's turn. Rome considered both countries interesting examples of mixed religions. It cherished a somewhat peculiar idea about bringing Roman Catholics together with orthodox Anglicans in England and with Protestants in Holland. It assumed that the Dutch Reformed Churches would collapse— a thought which was not wholly absent from the mind of some Dutch Catholics—and that out of the ruins Roman Catholicism, so admirably faithful for such a long time, would rise triumphant and gradually recover the place it had lost. It is true that Dutch Protestantism at that time was passing through a phase of inward division and theologically opposite movements.

Could you briefly describe the significance of the process of emancipation?

The process of emancipation lasted for about a century and has only now reached completion. It can be described as the growth towards maturity of a whole closely-knit group of the population. It has been such an intensive development that sociologists consider it as something out of the ordinary: after all, it began when the entire country still had less than three million inhabitants, of whom about eight hundred thousand were Catholic, whilst today there are more than twelve million inhabitants with more than five million Catholics. Much of the present prestige of Dutch Catholicism derives from this emancipation process. It brought excellent Catholic dailies and periodicals among which *De Tijd*, a Catholic daily, covered the whole period and helped to shape it. Led by Herman Schaepman, priest, orator and poet, the Catholics were moulded into one large political party without which the political system could not work. It was customary for parish priests to encourage their parishioners from the pulpit to vote for 'our own party'. From that time dates the expression 'the Roman cause' which every Catholic was supposed to cherish. The most prominent facet of this 'cause' was, for our ancestors, the financial and juridical parity of Catholic education with state education. This aim was reached

B

even before the twentieth century, and Catholics made many sacrifices for it. The best that parents could give to their children was a sound Catholic education. These views were shared by the Protestants who joined their brethren in Christ (while they continued to treat each other as heretics) in the battle for an Education Act to give equal opportunity to all. Even today private (the Dutch prefer to call it 'special') education of Catholics and Protestants is still more powerful than public (state) education. The same can be said of nursing, two-thirds of which is still in Catholic hands. Tens of thousands of religious have distinguished themselves in the fields of education and nursing.

What about social progress?

The rise of Catholic social organizations has been of incalculable importance. This social progress happened in Holland years after it had begun in the surrounding countries, partly because industrialization made a belated start. Many Catholics thought for a long time that charity was enough to cope with social needs and injustice. It was again the priests who gave the lead; this was logical because they were the intellectual leaders of Catholics.

The social encyclical *Rerum Novarum* produced, in the early years of the century, a new generation of priests with progressive ideas. One of them, Alfons Ariëns, fragile, shy, but full of fire, confronted the situation and managed, through his personal magnetism, to unite Catholic labourers in a workers' organization of their own. He was followed by Hendrik Poels who did the same for the Catholic miners. In all this the still socially deprived Catholic worker had no reason to be disappointed in his Church leaders. Thanks to this active apostolate of certain priests the Catholic workers were never lost to the Church. The struggle for social justice was therefore by no means the exclusive preserve of socialists. Yet one may well ask whether without the socialists there would have been such a determined effort to achieve a just distribution of the goods of this earth; for most of this Catholic activity was principally inspired by the defensive desire to prevent the 'loss of souls'. While the clergy did not have much influence on the workers who had immigrated from the provinces to the two great cities of Amsterdam and Rotterdam, their efforts had nevertheless proved that industrialization need not necessarily mean loss of faith and leaving the Church. Among other things, the result has been that Catholics are firmly represented today at every social and professional level.

The reverse of the coin is that religious isolation was maintained and that the country came to be divided into more or less sharply defined groups. This isolation produced prejudice and narrow-mindedness. Anybody with different opinions was suspect. There was no need to have an opinion of one's own since opinions were provided by the ecclesiastical leaders. The individual who dared to think 'differently' was soon cold-shouldered and subjected to contempt and labelled as a heretic. Intolerance, short-sightedness and conceit were not exactly alien to this sectarian way of life, in spite of its undoubtedly fruitful and protective elements. It spread into every kind of activity—there was even a Catholic organization for the breeding of goats!

Was there any improvement in the relations with Protestants?

The restoration of the hierarchy was a most unpleasant affair. The text, drafted in Rome, for the papal proclamation was adorned with quite fantastic diplomatic blunders. Holland at that time was still considered a Protestant nation, and here came the papal brief from an already suspect Rome, which talked of 'heretical Calvinism' and other such expressions. There were riots and bloodshed in 1853. A wave of anti-popery washed over the Low Countries, and flooded it with pamphlets, protest demonstrations, letters to the king and similar manifestations. The Protestants were afraid of an invasion of ultramontane, anti-patriotic bishops who would only pay tribute to Rome. The old fear of the inquisition emerged again and was to remain prominent for the rest of that century. Protestants looked on the 'Romans' as bandits emerging from the monasteries through subterranean passages in order to raid the country or kidnap little Protestant children to throw them into pits of quick-lime. The distrust was mutual and obstinate. The ecumenical movement, in which Holland now occupies a leading position, could therefore never have started there: its origins must be looked for in the mission countries of the Commonwealth.

*In this light, emancipation appears as a social process which
highlighted certain flaws in the spiritual or religious maturing
of the faithful. Why was this?*

The social and political equality of Catholics with the rest of the
population was not really fully achieved until after the second
world war. It was only then that Catholic organizations sought
and found viable contacts with other groups. Catholic education
had borne fruit and, years after the Protestants had already set up
their own university, a special effort was made to establish the
Catholic University of Nijmegen. Gradually there emerged a
Catholic intellectual laity. This phenomenon drove the priests
from their outposts back to their pastoral function. There arose
criticism of the old, closed and too clerical character of the situation. Catholic publicity, backed by new Catholic papers such as
Volkskrant, and already well-developed, created a broadly-based
Catholic radio which penetrated into every household and every
presbytery with its formative and unifying programmes.

Culturally the new awakening was inaugurated at the end of the
nineteenth century by Alberdink Thijm, businessman and author,
who made Catholics aware of their great medieval past. The
architect, A. Cuypers, filled the wide, green landscape with high
neo-Gothic churches whose artistically successful triumphalism
reacted against the still prevalent inferiority complex of Catholics.
There was an increase in self-confidence, but the actual practice
of the faith was still very inward-looking and not devoid of a
certain contempt for the profane world.

*Were Catholics of that period aware of this religious
immaturity?*

The enthusiasm of that period was genuine and spontaneous, and
a little infantile. One was jubilant because the parish priest had
said there was cause of jubilation. The First Vatican Council
dealt, among other things, with the primacy and infallibility of
the pope. This roused some opposition in the years before the
Council and at the Council itself. There was none of this
opposition in Holland where the new dogmas were hauled in with
colours flying, nor did the Dutch bishops play any part

whatsoever at that Council. All this may have been influenced by
the political leader, Herman Schaepman, who welcomed with
flowing oratory anything that concerned the pope or descended
from Rome. When the Papal States were threatened by the
revolutionary Garibaldi, Dutch Catholics saw this as pure sacri-
lege. There was a genuine mood of war in the air and this introduced a mysterious period in Dutch Church history, the episode
of the Zouaves.

*Does this episode not show that the Dutch are not always as
cool-headed as is sometimes said?*

Pio Nono begged the world to send soldiers to defend the Papal
States. The response was poor except in Holland where some
3,000 young men girded themselves for the 'holy war', and
in France, which contributed the same number to the total of
11,000 Zouaves that constituted the papal army. They were ready
to lay down their lives for the Pope. Strange to say, this enthusiasm was not in the least inspired by the Dutch bishops. Even they
looked askance at this 'psychotic Romanism'. The explanation
lies probably in the attractive personality of Pio Nono himself,
whose portrait decorated the walls of about three-quarters of the
Catholic homes. Pio Nono had restored the hierarchy, and even a
Protestant poet spoke of him as other worldly, 'his noble head
covered with the snow of age'. In short, Dutch Catholics thought
and acted with eyes and ears trained on Rome. Their inferiority
complex shows in this: in their local isolation they felt a strong
need for the moral support of a world-embracing Mother Church.

*Does this ultramontane fever also explain the colossal missionary
effort of the Dutch?*

This missionary zeal seems to be of a much purer metal. This
may be seen in the fact that even today over five thousand Dutch
priests are labouring in missions all over the world, giving
one of the most authentic proofs of the genuine faith and practice
of Dutch Catholicism. And this has been so for three-quarters of
a century. This Dutch effort has never been influenced by political
motives. Nor can one maintain that the missionaries were simply
good-natured adventurers who suffered from claustrophobia in

their small country since this missionary ideal permeated every
milieu, and was strongest in the small villages with their simple,
hard-working inhabitants.

They also remained attached, in a most moving manner, to
their place of origin, which is understandable since it was from
this enthusiastic home-front that they received money and goods,
letters and encouragement. The fact that Protestants also started
missionary work, particularly in Indonesia, was no doubt a stimulus but even that never became a determining factor. The lively
interest in the missions may perhaps owe something to the seminary training provided by the various mission congregations
which was far less expensive than that of the secular seminaries.
The fact remains that many young men dreamt of missionary
ideals and that parents saw there a career of the highest nobility.

*In the meantime, isolation and emancipation had already
continued over several generations, and in the period between
the two world wars there was a kind of ghetto-mentality. This
period is often ironically described as that of the 'rich Roman
life'. Most Catholics over thirty have experienced something of
this, some even a great deal. The young people hear of it from
their parents or in the documentary writings of Michel van der
Plas, which deal with that period and are very popular. Was
this period then so oppressive that it is so emphatically rejected
today?*

The 'rich Roman life' extolled those families that were blessed
with many children, preferably ten or more. One of these at least
was expected to become a priest and one of the daughters at least
should abandon the world and enter a convent. The happiest day
of a Catholic's life was when, in reward for his many services, he
would receive the papal decoration *Pro Ecclesia et Pontifice* (For
Church and Pope). The boys played football in Catholic clubs
and learned to complain about the rough play of non-Catholic
boys. The girls could not find a better preparation for
motherhood than in a Catholic domestic science school and by
frequenting with their sisters the weekly meetings of the Children
of Mary.

To go to the early Mass at least three times a week was a

minimal moral obligation for every youngster, and the teacher marked down each one's performance in order to fill in the totals on the school report. The most abominable inroad into this blessed enclosure was of course a mixed marriage, against which fierce prayers were sent up to heaven from every home and every church. On his way through home and school, through youth club and Catholic union the Catholic had at his disposal an endless stream of pious literature. This frequently praised somewhat obscure young saints, exhorted him to prayer and to the reception of the sacraments. A climax was achieved when in a book or magazine some dramatic story ended with a death-bed conversion.

The commandments, divine or ecclesiastical—no difference was made between these—were not infrequently buried under a load of scruples which, as often as not, came dangerously close to magic or superstition. Today one would be embarrassed by this opulent exhibition of smugness and middle-class self-sufficiency, were it not that these same good church-goers were capable of an almost monumental spirit of self-sacrifice and zeal for the good cause. This can still be found, unspoiled, in the fields of education and the missions, and in the many Catholic organizations.

Surely people gradually began to feel the need for a more personal and critical approach to the great issues.

One must point out that modernism, which had already become an important problem in several European countries, never had a firm foothold in Holland. Theology was considered complete and fixed as a science, and the modern developments in philosophy and technology, as well as the discoveries about evolution, were taken as so many sacrilegious attacks on this theology. One may say that the great problems thrown up by modernism were not touched for more than half a century and only came in, so to speak, by stealth. The same can be said of the tendency towards independent thought—I am not speaking here of the subjectivism which, since the Reformation, had threatened to divide the faithful into groups wherein each claimed the monopoly of the orthodox faith, but rather the desire to approach the essential matters of faith from every single angle.

Who were the critics and what did they want?

They were mainly ex-students for the priesthood who were active in the various arts. They were young and soon outgrew the widespread cultural pessimism inspired by *The Decline of the West*. These young Catholics were most aware of the sterile atmosphere in their own surroundings, where Catholics as a whole were still glorying in their own merits. These merits were no doubt real but offered no guarantee whatever for a live faith and a true humanity. The opposition went to work against the little narrow world which previous generations had built for themselves and which they had surrounded with impenetrable ramparts. From within, it looked all very comfortable: one could, in obvious unison, play Catholic football, breed Catholic goats, indulge in Catholic politics and remain fixed in a Catholic blindness to the needs and worries outside.

In 1925, these young people launched their own magazine, *De Gemeenschap* (The Community), and their most prominent spokesman was an author-journalist who wrote under the name of Anton van Duinkerken. He laid bare the outward appearances which hid so little substance, and attacked the empty slogans of the conformists. He demanded that the windows should be thrown open and fresh air let in. Christianity did not consist in a nervous and cowardly withdrawal from the world. He broached the great issues in polemics that were eagerly followed. He was supported by a group of young, artistically gifted Catholics but the clerical theologians remained outside, and this was enough to condemn the movement in the eyes of the simple faithful. From within the fortress there came cries of 'Scandal!' and the criticism was branded as an assault on everything that was good and holy. There was no worse magazine, they said, than *De Gemeenschap*, which was, inevitably, forbidden literature for all seminarians. But this public condemnation could not diminish the attractive persuasiveness of its writing, and the new generation of priests secretly passed it on from hand to hand. It was more openly discussed by the Catholic students of Nijmegen, as well as those of Utrecht, Amsterdam and Leiden, where small student organizations were less prejudiced, more open-minded.

Apart from a few individual cases, there was no open rift. The conformist majority sought to eliminate *De Gemeenschap* by ignoring it. Among themselves they were agreed that these young hotheads took inadmissible liberties with the true faith and they cheerfully tried to blacken the honest intentions of the young.

It must be admitted that many priests found it difficult to stomach this invasion by the laity of the privileged fields of theology and philosophy, the more so as these layfolk were frequently better equipped than those who had had no more than a limited seminary training. But the artificial element in clerical authority was decently disposed of, and one must definitely grant that later on they adjusted themselves admirably to the changed situation.

During the second world war this new awakening, stirred up by *De Gemeenschap*, lay fallow for several years. The worries created by the German occupation concerned life and death, freedom and imprisonment. Domestic quarrels were quenched, and with fairly general unity and under the courageous leadership of Archbishop De Jong, Catholics now turned against the German occupiers and the persecutors of the Jews.

How did the second world war affect the situation?

During the years before the war there was a troublesome vague inclination towards fascism among a number of young Catholics, though not among those who followed *De Gemeenschap*. And obviously, not everyone was clearly aware of all the implications of fascism. The misleading line taken by Vatican diplomacy in favour of Franco during the Spanish civil war went uncorrected through lack of careful explanation in Holland. Fascism's resolute character and demand for action (sparing nothing, as was to become clear later on) appealed to some in a time that was marked by political paralysis. Fortunately, most of those who 'strayed' changed their minds completely once they encountered fascism as embodied in the Nazis. In any case the Dutch bishops and clergy never compromised with the *Heil Hitler* movement as the German hierarchy did. They publicly and forcefully protested against Nazi injustice. The war turned Dutch Catholics into good patriots, something that had been in doubt before the war because of ultramontane inclinations.

They took part in the underground resistance movement, together with Protestants and Communists. These contacts, forged by the desperate circumstances, were of immense importance. Much of the ecumenical contact today dates from that period of war. Numerous young people, hidden in secret corners, discussed things together and dreamt of a new post-war society, when Protestants, Catholics and Socialists would work together for a happier future. Night after night they worked out the most breath-taking plans for post-war days.

Was this the after-effect of the Gemeenschap *movement?*

This movement was only one of the factors. There were many similar-minded youngsters who refused to revert to the dull and colourless pre-war situation.

What happened to these fine ideals?

The ideals proved illusory. The progressive young Catholics remained small in number, while the conservative-minded remained just as numerous as before. This latter group immediately set to work on restoring the pre-war situation, openly encouraged by the bishops: they brought back the Catholic political party, Catholic organizations and clubs, the solid principles of our ancestors, etc. All was, of course, to be modernized and adjusted to the new age, but the hour of a breakthrough towards a new set-up had not yet come. As before, it was a matter of 'prudent government', 'really solid discussion', 'we must proceed step by step', and so on. The young progressives did not stand a chance and out of protest broke with the Catholic party, launched their own magazine and refused to accept functions in Catholic organizations.

The continued insistence on a policy of isolation meant that people thought or acted only according to their denominational label. Catholic continued to keep apart from Protestant, and socialist from liberal (in Holland this denotes a broadminded conservative, not an English 'liberal'). This was the basis of the Dutch set-up. This is the 'establishment' (*zuilenstelsel*) and if there is

anything totally incomprehensible in Holland it is this system of
partitions between people in literally every field. Yet one must
admit that somehow it manages to function for all its drawbacks.

In 1953 the Dutch bishops announced that Catholics had to
remain within their own Catholic organizations. They also gave
it as their opinion that Catholic interests were best preserved by
the Catholic political party and the Catholic labour movement.
This statement by the hierarchy created a great stir. Many
disagreed but the majority obeyed its directives.

To the Catholic of today this all seems very long ago. The
statement is no longer valid. In many ways it never was. When,
for instance, it urged Catholics not to listen to the socialist radio,
this proved too much for most people. Before the second world
war it was still the custom in Catholic homes to switch the radio
off as soon as the voice of a Protestant pastor could be heard,
but even then one got more than tired of listening to a long
series of preaching priests and religious. Precisely because
television, supported by the establishment, ignored the fears implied in the statement of the bishops, it contributed greatly to
better mutual understanding and the breaking down of the rusty
partitions.

The isolation policy is gone now. After a century of 'training'
the Dutch Catholic is supposed to be adult enough to listen to
other opinions. The union among Catholics which was meant to
serve as a support at every step forward, has remained as strong
as before. Social relations have not suffered in any way, and the
various groups of the population have learned to appreciate one
another, which has made for better co-operation.

It is debatable whether this determined isolation policy had to
be maintained so long. Is not the unbridgeable gulf between
progressive and conservative Catholics precisely one of its worst
effects? This gulf has created an impoverishment of the spirit on
both sides. Now we have to pay the price for it as innovators
brutally break with tradition and the traditionalists sink more and
more deeply in the morass of their isolation because they cannot
lower themselves to shaking hands with those who want to go
ahead.

*This last question tries to link up again with our first one, which
asked with what in the past of Dutch Catholicism the present
crisis can be compared. If there is so much now that reminds
one of the Reformation, does this mean that history is
repeating itself? In other words, is there any reason to fear a
separation, a tragic schism between Rome and Dutch Catholicism?*

There is no such danger. The Reformation has been a lesson for
all and for all time. In Holland as in the universal Church one is
fully aware that on no account must we ever again let it come to
that. It should not have happened then, but the brakes were not
as strong as they are today. At that time society was thinly
populated, mainly agricultural and not culturally mature. Now
this society is thickly populated and, through industrialization,
closely interdependent. In such a situation public opinion does not
suddenly change course. Compared with that time, present
society leaves room for a great variety of thought, and institutions
are much more widely developed, so that dogmatism, rigidity
and centralized government are bound to have less of a hold. But
let us cease this kind of speculation. It is rather meaningless.

3. VATICAN II AND THE DUTCH CATHOLICS

MICHEL VAN DER PLAS

When Pope John XXIII declared his intention to summon an Ecumenical Council on 25 January 1959, the reaction of the Dutch Catholics was the same as that of all other Catholics all over the world: they were taken by surprise. Most had more or less forgotten that there had been numerous councils in the Church's history. Those who knew better thought the chances of a new Council after that of 1870 too small to be taken seriously. Only an isolated individual like the great social pioneer Dr. Poels had been ruminating in the recent past on the desirability of a new Council, in his long correspondence with Muckermann.

In Holland, as almost everywhere else, Pope John was looked on simply as a 'transition pope'. When the cry *'Habemus papam'* (we have a pope) went up in St Peter's Square in the autumn of 1958, many found it difficult to hide their disappointment that it was Angelo Roncalli who had been chosen. When, in 1965, I asked a Dutch priest who for twenty years had been a professor at the Papal University in Rome what he found the most painful moment in all that time he answered: 'That afternoon of 28 October. I then thought, all is lost, this cannot be the pope the Church needed.' He still wondered occasionally, with a shake of his head, how he could have been so mistaken.

It did not take long for the Dutch Catholics to get accustomed to the Pope and the purpose which dominated the end of his life. One may even say that it was this Council which almost revolutionarily changed the Church of Holland, both inwardly and outwardly. It seemed to make its bishops, priests and laity suddenly articulate, and all at the same level. It was jerked into a new awareness of its own character among the other provinces of the Church. The Council precipitated a spontaneous shaking off of religious attitudes, spirituality and ways of life, inherited from

45

the period of the 'rich Roman life'. Towards the end some saw a
bitter element of truth in one of those 'Council jokes': 'What is
the difference between a missionary in Africa and a bishop in
Holland?—The missionary makes wild men Catholic, the bishop
makes Catholic men wild.'

One may say in general that, after the new Council had been
publicized and explained in a clear and often interesting manner
to the people through numerous publications, the daily, weekly
and monthly press, and the excellent letter of the hierarchy of
Christmas 1960, it was felt as a liberation throughout the Dutch
Church. While theologians, moralists, exegetes and Church
historians were hoping for a period of 'thaw' after the ice age
that had seemed to follow the appearance of the encyclical
Humani generis, and pastors began to see broader possibilities for
a more modern approach to their work, hampered as it was by
restlessness, a small but influential group of lay people as well as
priests began to think aloud about a series of needs and
desiderata which the Council should tackle. Today one can see
that they were rather moderate, compared with what came out
during and after the Council in a kind of snowballing fashion.
Yet, even in the years 1959-62, there were already some who
considered the moderate Catholic as too bold and going too far.

This moderate Catholic still had to learn how to manipulate the
principle of free speech within the Church, although it should be
said that he learned it very quickly: it was not long before the
Archbishop of Utrecht began, still in the pre-conciliar period, to
plead for more moderation in criticism, less extreme wishes and a
less polemical tone. In any case, when Vatican II was opened on
11 October 1962 the Dutch Church already represented the most
passionately interested and best informed ecclesiastical province
in the universal Church.

Only future historians will be able to say how far the Dutch
hierarchy who, at the general request of Pope John to send in as
extensive a list of suggestions as possible, presented their *vota*
(wishes) in writing, fulfilled the repeated promise to listen to the
voice of the people of God. It would appear that it was only at a
later stage that the frequent and intensive contacts took place
between the bishops on the one hand and the clergy and laity on

the other which made the Dutch contribution to the Council a genuinely representative one. The question is whether the bishops could have sent in more and richer ideas (except for those connected with the document on the Church in the world), if this close consultation had already taken place in the preparatory period. When one reads the first list sent in by the hierarchy, one misses a genuinely positive approach especially in this field of Church and world, but this strikes one as common to the whole row of volumes contributed by all the national hierarchies.

Yet, in general, the contribution of the Dutch hierarchy makes a brisk and bright impression. In the documents that came from other countries one often meets with ideas that are almost alien to this age, extremely conservative, concerned with trivialities (one bishop can hardly think of anything better than what priests should wear when travelling: he was 'shocked' by what was going on); alongside this there is the lust for definition and the zeal for anathemas: there were altogether some ninety 'isms' put forward for condemnation, varying from 'pan-nudism' to Rotary Clubs. The Dutch bishops, on the other hand, demanded in the items of their extensive list discussion of almost all the subjects that in fact received extensive treatment in the four sessions of the Council. What strikes the reader is their emphasis on such points as: a new description of what the 'Church' is ('not in juridical terms but biblical ones'), a responsible revision of the phrase *extra ecclesiam nulla salus* (no salvation outside the Church), pluriformity within the Church, a public admission of guilt with regard to the separated Christians, an adequate circumscription of the powers of a bishop, an effective decentralization, reform and internationalization of the Roman Curia, care for laicized priests, the general priesthood of the faithful, many liturgical reforms, etc. Important also was the plea to allow non-Catholic Christian leaders to speak at the Council; they also warned strongly against speaking in condemnatory terms and urgently asked that God's inspiration and guidance in the other Christian Churches should be recognized.

These vota, in the preparatory phase, were meant for internal consumption, but at the end of 1960 they wrote a collective pastoral letter which was exceptionally detailed, open-minded and even inspiring. This Christmas pastoral letter, written and printed in a large edition almost two years before the opening of the Council, raised much commotion later on. The bishops dealt not so much with the various topics the Council should tackle as with an exposition of how, according to them, a Council should be built up and lived throughout the Church. Many of their ideas have become commonly accepted but at that time they sounded remarkably fresh and courageous. Interesting, for instance, and later creating some difficulties, were the ideas about the Church as the 'people of God', about the sense of faith and how far this is infallible, about the relationship between this collective sense of faith and ecclesiastical authority, about the infallibility of the pope as linked with the faith within the Church, and about the collegiality of the bishops.

Translated into many languages and spread in many countries, this pastoral letter threatened to lead to a row on the eve of the Council when in the summer of 1962 the Italian translation was withdrawn from the shops by request of the Holy Office. After Cardinal Alfrink had tried to obtain information about this in Rome, even from Pope John himself, it was said that some 'less perfect and somewhat unclear passages' had slipped into the translation. The initiated knew better: Roman theology, particularly that of the Lateran University, had serious objections to the new theological opinions which formed the basis of the pastoral letter, and saw to it that the letter was checked by the Holy Office for errors.

Unfortunately, the matter did not end there. Not only did the Holy Office drag out the investigation, even after the Council had been under way for a considerable time, but the theologian explicitly named and thanked at the end of the letter for his 'valuable help', Professor Schillebeeckx, was from that time suspect in Rome and had to serve as scapegoat. Although one of the half-dozen principal theologians of our time he, by exception, was not nominated as a *peritus* (official expert) of the Council (he was entitled to this nomination simply as expert for the Dutch hierarchy), and he became aware that there was an agent of the Holy Office present at every conference he gave during the Council. When, during the fourth session, he had held a conference in the Domus Mariae in Rome on the encyclical *Mysterium Fidei*, he was mentioned with almost explicit ridicule in the Council assembly itself by the general secretary, Archbishop Felici. Later on the Dutch Catholics would frequently have to face curial displeasure.

It is no exaggeration to say that when the Dutch hierarchy left for the Council in October 1962, they had everywhere except in their own country the reputation of being the most progressive. Whether they themselves were happy with this reputation is doubtful. Aware that they represented only one percent of Catholics in the world they did not visualize themselves as called upon to play a significant part; they merely wanted to be of service and in this they were not motivated by extreme nationalistic wishes but only by interest in the Church as a whole. Yet, when on the eve of the Council the Italian press called Cardinal Alfrink 'the rebel from the North', either his interventions in the Central Commission or some of his lectures must have attracted a great deal of attention for him to deserve such a name in Roman eyes. One particular idea of his had provoked wide discussion: namely, the wish that a more or less permanent advisory college of bishops should be created in Rome on the lines of the multi-national composition of the Central Commission – an idea that was later to take shape in the Synod of bishops. That this did not make him particularly popular with the Roman school of thought and their ideas about centralization is obvious.

Mention should be made of another important initiative taken in Holland by the late Bishop Bekkers. When, in the summer of 1962, the first conciliar schemata were circularized to the bishops he started (to quote Schillebeeckx who was very close to him) an 'offensive': as a simple bishop he hardly understood what the Council and the people of God should do with such documents, and so he invited some theologians to provide these texts with detailed commentaries and a series of question-marks; these were collected and published in an edition of 4,000 copies for distribution among the other bishops and their advisers, when they had arrived in Rome. Within a short time many other bishops followed this example so that for the rest of the Council all the bishops were provided with reactions to the draft texts as they were handed out, with beneficial results.

This leads me to another specifically Dutch contribution to Vatican II. On the whole, the Dutchman is rarely a great original thinker, but he is excellent at reading and assimilating the theories that float around. He can summarize them intelligently and spread them in a popularized and handy form, even if, for foreigners, somewhat clumsily, not very diplomatically, and rather stiffly. There is some truth in the quip which went round the Council: 'The truth? The Italians have it, the Spaniards defend it, the Germans make it complicated, the French analyze it, the Americans pay for it, and the Dutch print it.'

The fact is that during the first session the Dutch set up a purely Dutch foundation, called 'Documentation Centre for the Council', now better known as DOC. This provided the Council Fathers not only with weekly lectures, but particularly with duplicated 'papers' which contained for each subject under discussion an excellent documentation of the various theological opinions on the particular point at issue, as well as all kinds of factual information that formed the background to each issue. It may be said that DOC played a key part in the development of Vatican II.

Then the Council started in all seriousness. Within two sessions all seven bishops from Holland were members of one Commission or another; their theologians and secretaries co-ordinated many international activities and consultations outside the official meetings, and at home the 'domestic front' awaited the first results impatiently and critically. Perhaps many other ecclesiastical provinces experienced the same thing as the Dutch: impatient as people were at first while waiting for the concrete results, there was little enthusiasm left when the outcome of the first deliberations became known, and many were anxious that actual documents should be postponed till the issues had ripened somewhat. The intense interest with which Dutch Catholics followed the proceedings in Rome paved the way for wishful dreams which could perhaps only come true in a Third Vatican Council. At the same time their too keen expectations were bound to be damped to a certain extent. If I may anticipate the final effect of the Council I would say that in general there was, not infrequently, a gap between the conciliar assembly and the 'domestic front', between the subjects so often exhaustively and tiresomely dealt with in Rome and the urgent issues of which people became more and more acutely aware, between the prestige which the Church seemed to assume in Council and that which it actually has in this world.

It has been said that the reporters often gave undue emphasis to peripheral incidents rather than the real substance of the Council. In general this is just not true. On the other hand, things have been described as peripheral which both reporters and ordinary people instinctively understood to be of major historical importance and decisive for the breakthrough of a new theology, a new spirituality, a new attitude of the Church towards the world. There was, for instance, the rapidly emerging division of minds at the Council and the way the press rightly brought this out; there was the refusal by the assembly to accept the lists of candidates for Commissions prepared by the Curia; there were the sharp words addressed by Cardinal Frings to the Holy Office, and there were the many intrigues and conflicts in the background. People saw this instinctively as a purifying process, or at least the beginning of one, undertaken by the Council itself. Perhaps the Dutchman particularly was rather more passionately interested in these efforts to purge the Church of all kinds of insincerity, pomposity, narrow-mindedness, illiberality and even tyranny, than in the growth and final drafts of the conciliar documents. I believe that this partially successful process of purification has been both good and necessary, and that it was for many the condition for the acceptance, assimilation, elaboration and discussion of the more direct results—the Constitutions and Decrees.

It had, of course, to be the Dutch Cardinal Alfrink who, during the first session, on 30 October 1962, made a gesture which, innocent and well enough meant in itself, was taken at once as symbolical and historic by a press that was still nervously casting about for news and by people who were waiting for some token of a decisive breakthrough: after having warned Cardinal Ottaviani that the time-limit for his speech had run out, he simply

stopped him and received loud applause for this—to his own
surprise. It was a typically Dutch gesture, unemotional, to the
point and not terribly diplomatic, and it was ironical that it was
once again that 'rebel from the North' who seemed to personify
the opposition.

But the contribution made by the Dutch hierarchy has been far
more constructive than that. Although the other Dutch bishops
spoke up firmly in the decisive debates and always on the side of
'renewal', the interventions by Cardinal Alfrink must be considered the most important, and some deserve to be mentioned
here. What he said was usually sober, clear and typical of a man
with scientific training, which is perhaps why his views were so
respected and influential. Moreover, during the sessions and
between them he held an unusual number of conferences in
Holland and abroad in which he explained and enlarged upon his
interventions in the assembly. In this he emphasized particularly
the individual character of the various peoples and the right and
duty of these people to express this character in the manner in
which they practise their faith. Unity-in-diversity should be the
important new mark of the Church today and in the future.

During the debates in St Peter's the Cardinal spoke more
from behind the presidential table, as the sessions became longer
and more numerous. Most important was his intervention on 2
October 1963, when he mooted the relationship between pope
and bishops in the debate on the schema on the Church. He
fastened on to the expression used in the draft: 'Peter and the
apostles':

'This manner of speaking about Peter and the apostles sounds
strange and unusual because one might understand it to
mean that Peter was not an apostle. This does not do
justice to Peter. On the contrary, he is the principal apostle
because he has a place within the college of apostles, and even
the first place. I would therefore suggest that we read "Peter
and the other apostles", or "Peter with the other apostles." ...
When we speak about "Peter with the other apostles", we affirm
two things: first, that Peter has a place within the college of
apostles, and second, that in this college Peter occupies a
special, extraordinary and noble place, because he is named

separately. Such a way of speaking, therefore, does not make Peter equal to the other apostles, but links them together, while at the same time indicating Peter's special place. [Then, with a reference to Matthew 16:17 and Revelation 21:14, he continued] We have two biblical images with different, significant terms. On the one hand, Peter and Peter alone is the *petra*, the rock on which Christ built his Church. On the other, the Church has twelve foundations, *i.e.*, the twelve apostles as the apostolic college which bears the Church in its own way.'

Here he gave an important biblical and theological foundation for the collegiality of the bishops which Vatican II was later to proclaim.

A second important intervention concerned the function of the bishops and reflected the Cardinal's own ideas: a permanent council of bishops gathered round the pope. This, he said, would not be identical with the whole body of bishops, nor would it represent that college in a parliamentary sense. This central organism would be

'a sign of the collegial government of the Church ... and moreover at the same time a means by which this collegial government of the Church could be exercised in a definite way. Thus it would also show the highest power in the Church. Such a central organ would show the unity of the Church and in a definite way promote the "centralization" of the Church's government. . . . Moreover, such a central organ would strengthen mutual confidence between the centre of the Church and the distant regions. [And about the place of the Roman Curia, he added] Seen from this angle, the place of the Roman Curia will not be *between* the Holy Father and the bishops who are spread all over the world, but it should serve the college of bishops. Within the Church of Christ the order must not be: first the Holy Father, then the Roman Curia and in the third place the bishops. If the collegiality of the bishops is of divine right, the order must be: the Holy Father, who, with the other bishops of the Church, forms the college of bishops, and then the Roman Curia, as the executive organ of

this body of bishops (although at the same time serving the
Holy Father himself as pope).'

This distinction was obviously of major importance since in the
past the Roman Curia had too often looked upon itself as the
'long arm' of the pope, and criticism of its methods was identified
with criticism of the pope.

In connection with this debate about the Church the Cardinal
also made an important contribution to the revised schema on
Mary which, after long debates, was to end up as the last chapter
of the Constitution on the Church instead of being promulgated
as a separate document. Among the bishops there was constant
talk about 'maximalists' and 'minimalists', and one of the ways of
deciding who belonged to what was to see whether a bishop
agreed with or rejected a whole series of titles with which Mary
would be credited in this schema. At the end, tired with it all,
Alfrink intervened on 18 September 1964 in unusually forceful
terms:

'My conscience forces me to speak out here in this assembly to
the honour of our Lord Jesus Christ and the honour of the
blessed Virgin Mary.'

He argued that the only thing that mattered in this chapter was
to indicate

'what *all* faithful of the Catholic Church must accept. This
chapter is not concerned with what one thinks *within* the
Church but with what is taught and must be taught *by* the
Church. . . . On this point there is no room for talk about
minimalism and maximalism. When we talk about devotion,
which may be great or little, or about the various opinions of
theologians and other faithful, then, indeed, we may dis-
tinguish between minimalists and maximalists. But when we
talk about the faith of the Church and what the Church must
teach, we are only and exclusively dealing with the true faith of
the Church which does not allow of a "greater" or "lesser" but
only of what is true.'

On this basis, among others, he thought that the title of 'Mary
Mediatrix' was unsuited to the draft that was being discussed.

A third subject which the Cardinal dealt with in a wholly
typical manner and on behalf of all the Dutch bishops was the

clergy. In the autumn of 1964 he mentioned celibacy and gave the following warning:

'This Council cannot ignore the crisis which has arisen in this matter in many different places. Even if the Council cannot solve all the problems, the Fathers should make it clear that they are aware of these problems and recognize them. The connection between celibacy and priesthood should be based on a biblical foundation and seen in the light of tradition, taking account of the difficulties of this age and the modern mentality. And perhaps the Church might add something to this schema that could console and strengthen those of our priests who find celibacy a burden.'

Almost a year later the general secretary, Archbishop Felici, read out a letter from the Pope, saying that he did not deem a public debate on celibacy desirable in the assembly.

Through their leader, the Dutch bishops made several notable contributions to the debate about the relations of the Church with the modern world. In connection with the chapter on marriage and family, the Cardinal pointed to the difficulties which many married persons experienced in the fulfilment of the moral duties of their state.

'The Church always teaches that sacrifice and self-denial belong to the essence of Christianity. Not only the cross, however, but also the joy of the resurrection belongs to the essence of Christianity and God has no joy in the suffering of men. . . . The new knowledge brought about by anthropology and the growing understanding of the difference between mere bio-logical sexuality and human sexuality raise an *honest doubt* in many married couples as well as among scientists and several theologians, at least in connection with the arguments adduced to prove that in such conflicts in married life total or periodical abstention is the only totally effective, moral and Christian solution for faithful of goodwill. The situation is so serious that the Church must not solve this real problem with a hasty and perhaps immature decision. . . . Only when there is genuine certainty about the real content of divine law can the Church bind or release the conscience of the faithful. [This he followed up with the plea that] a permanent commission should be set up of experts in philosophy, theology and the sciences, which must keep in step with scientific development in view of pastoral care, in order to prevent the Church from ever being too late in discerning new problems.'

In the debate of this same schema the Cardinal sharply rejected any solemn condemnation of communism, asked for by a minority. He pointed out that this had already been made repeatedly by popes and bishops, and demanded that the dialogue with communism should be encouraged. It was true that the attempt at a dialogue 'with official representatives of atheistic communism on basic issues had always been in vain', but experts maintained that 'a personal discussion with men of goodwill, although convinced communists, had led, more than once, to a repetition of the nocturnal conversation of Christ with Nicodemus'.

At a somewhat later stage the Cardinal spoke out on the questions of the arms race and the so-called 'just war'. With regard to the first he insisted that the projected pastoral constitution should not be less firm on this point than *Pacem in Terris*. On the second issue he demanded with the same force that the so-called 'clean' bomb should be condemned as much as the so-called 'dirty' one. He added:

'One may well ask in this connection whether the old theory of a just and an unjust war should be mentioned as was done in para. 2 of n. 25. This formulation seems to suggest that this Council declares that one can indeed think of a war where the use of nuclear weapons etc. can be justified. I doubt whether any one of us means this.... The question which worries everybody is not whether atomic war can be allowed in one way or another; the greatest worry of all mankind is that there ever should be an atomic war.'

Space prevents me from mentioning a series of other interventions by the Dutch hierarchy on subjects such as revelation, the missions and the liturgy. In general one may say that these, like those I have quoted, were always efforts to ensure that, with a realistic view of a fast-changing society, the new understanding of modern theology should prevail over those traditional opinions which had proved inadequate for our times.

One gets the impression that, as the Council proceeded, the Dutch bishops took more and more note of what their own people suggested and that they adopted these suggestions in their own personal interventions. There was here a very happy exchange between hierarchy and people with the result that, at home, people recognized their own ideas in what the bishops said in Rome.

All, however, was by no means quiet on the home front as the Council proceeded. Opinions on the Council were somewhat emotional, sometimes highly critical or sceptical. This did not exactly ease the position of the hierarchy. Eyebrows of fellow-bishops in Rome were raised higher and higher at the news of some statement or other or some daring gesture made in their ecclesiastical province. Many an outsider was already surprised at the passionate interest of the Dutch faithful, an interest that was sometimes expressed in nervous telegrams addressed to the bishops at critical moments such as the publication of the apostolic constitution *Veterum sapientia* or the so-called 'Black Week'.

Among other groups of bishops Catholic Holland got the reputation of running wild, and of wanting to go further than the Council could or would. On the other hand, some instances of successful Dutch obstinacy were discussed in the world press and made a great impression on public opinion, which had in any case begun to understand more clearly the point of principles such as decentralization and pluriformity. Perhaps nowhere was attention so sharply focused on the Roman Curia as in Holland where its image was that of a collection of Italians who were out of touch with the world, congenital intriguers, people who tried to block any renewal in the Church, however sensible.

Just before the Council opened in 1962, Fr J. van Kilsdonk, S.J., moderator of the students at Amsterdam University, addressed the St Adelbertvereniging (the Dutch counterpart of the English Newman Association) and made a sharp attack on the Curia. He maintained that many Dutch Catholics lapsed largely because of the reactionary attitude of that Curia. After Cardinal Alfrink had publicly criticized this view as too absolute, the Holy Office reacted by demanding that van Kilsdonk be dismissed from his post. This provoked a storm of protest in Holland. Perturbed by this, but also because he was personally convinced that as the local ordinary he was fully capable of taking any necessary disciplinary measures, the Bishop of Haarlem, Monsignor van Dodewaard, sought and obtained an interview with Cardinal Ottaviani. The result was surprising: on 2 January 1963, the Bishop published a statement in which he said that the Holy Office maintained its objections, but continued; 'In view of the fact that the Dutch authorities have already taken steps and taking note of the reaction to this address, the Holy Office leaves any further measures to the local bishop.' What were these further measures? At the end of his statement the Bishop of Haarlem informed the people that he was retaining Fr. van Kilsdonk as moderator of the students.

This precedent made one wonder whether the Holy Office would react so precipitately in future to whatever might happen to displease it in the Dutch province. A short time afterwards it had to climb down again in an equally startling case, when it was obliged publicly to rehabilitate a person it had unjustly condemned. This case concerned a woman psychiatrist, Dr A. Terruwe, who had been accused in 1950 of having ignored the laws of Catholic morality in the exercise of her profession (she frequently gave psychiatric advice to seminarians and priests). In spite of the investigation instituted by the Dutch bishops at that time and its conclusion, forwarded to Rome, that there was no foundation for these accusations against Dr Terruwe, the Holy Office set up an investigation of its own, through its consultant, Fr Tromp, S.J., and published an instruction which forbade seminarians, priests and religious to seek the advice of women psychiatrists.

The Dutch hierarchy protested in vain. Only when the Council was already far advanced could Cardinal Alfrink tell his people that

'the Holy Office had pointed out to him that, at its investigation, it was primarily concerned with opinions and methods which worried the Holy Office, not with persons. Therefore the Holy Office had waived fresh interrogations of certain persons after its previous investigations. The Holy Office also meant to avoid mentioning names in this connection. If Dr Terruwe's reputation has been hurt, the Holy Office wishes to express its regrets.'

This was, diplomatically, a very clever retraction, but the case constituted a novelty in modern Church history; it had happened before that the Holy Office had to rehabilitate persons, but this had always been done quietly. This time it had to do so publicly, and many began to realize the implications of this fact and that publicity can be an effective means of fostering honesty within the Church. It looked as if here lay the first-fruits of a re-appreciation of the bishop's power and dignity, and a rehabilitation of the local ordinary as judge in matters which lie within his competence.

Such cases, however, did not help to improve the relations between Dutch public opinion and 'Rome'. The daily and weekly Italian press developed a tendency to attack Dutch Catholics and their bishops, which soon lost all sense of proportion. Idiotic reports which gave a totally false image of the situation in Holland were printed. There were particularly exaggerated and alarming reports about apostasy among the Dutch clergy and about theories and practices connected with the Eucharist. It was even said that nothing less than a schism was on the verge of breaking out in 'the misty lowlands near the sea'.

The atmosphere was tense on both sides when the fourth and last session of the Council was about to begin. On the eve of this session Paul VI published his encyclical *Mysterium Fidei* on the Eucharist. The Italian press immediately suggested that it was aimed mainly at the heretical new opinions current in Holland. Papers like *Il Messagero*, *Il Giornale d'Italia*, *Il Tempo* and *Il Corriere* declared that the Pope had in mind the threatening schism in Holland. *Il Tempo*, of 12 September 1965, carried a headline: 'Paul VI condemns the deviations of the Dutch Church in his encyclical.' It is certain that this suggestion, that the encyclical was aimed principally at the Dutch Church, came from within the Vatican immediately before and after the publication of the text, and it is not exaggerated to say that this campaign against Holland was fostered by some prelates in the Vatican. In November the Italian writer, Dolcino Favi, wrote in the periodical *Questitalia* that the publication of the encyclical meant to 'let the Council end in a spirit of the most bitter lust for revenge on the part of the Curia'. The members of the Curia 'wanted to intimidate the Fathers effectively and particularly to discredit the Dutch bishops who, by their courageous attitude, had assumed the moral leadership of a majority and thus had to take increasing note of the opposition'. Favi showed that 'practically the whole Curia' had been concerned in this anti-Dutch propaganda, long before the publication of the encyclical.

One may well wonder whether the Dutch bishops did in fact assume the moral leadership with which Favi credits them. Fellow bishops often doubted whether a hierarchy in whose province sometimes things were said or done that seemed to conflict with orthodoxy and the usual respect for authority, deserved the title of 'leader'. On the other hand, one should realize that during the tiring sessions, with their constantly changing theological topics, many bishops who were themselves not too well-versed in the new theology would be inclined to let their opinions and votes be influenced by colleagues who had so often been proved right where pastoral insight was concerned. To this one should add that, in reality, there were not just seven Dutch bishops at the Council, but seventy, since the very large share of the Dutch in missionary work meant that very many mission bishops were Dutch (by birth), and these obviously let themselves be advised by Dutch theologians and advisers. And so it happened that some remarkable interventions came, for instance, from the Indonesian bishops Staverman and Geise, who really drew their water from the Dutch well. Nor was it mere chance that Monsignor Koop, the Brazilian bishop who, during the last session, had sent in a disturbing written intervention on the shortage of priests and propounded a radical solution of the problem, was again a Dutchman by birth. And so our country appeared with capital letters in the Curia's black book, and the Curia stooped so low as to air their anti-Dutch feelings in the presence of Italian journalists. The bomb of *Mysterium Fidei*, when it exploded in the press, was a carefully placed time-bomb.

Cardinal Alfrink, already for long the victim of a slander campaign in papers like *Il Tempo, Il Borghese, Il Giornale d'Italia*, and who was even said to behave unworthily, disrespectfully, etc., at certain liturgical ceremonies, took a courageous decision: he called a press conference at the *DOC* centre to present a defence of the Dutch Church, an event without precedent in Rome. On 15 September he said in a large hall, crammed with people: 'I hope you will forgive me if I say something nice here about the Dutch Catholics.' He said he knew very well what happened there, their failures, and that 'occasionally they said things that were not completely acceptable', but that he had no intention of 'restricting the opportunities for open discussion'. What he protested against was the allegation

'that the Catholic community of Holland was infected with an anti-Roman mentality. If this word means "anti-papal" I can quietly and categorically deny this. The contrary is true. But if we mean by that word that certain people in that Dutch community have a number of objections, perhaps sometimes fiercely expressed, against certain methods used by the Roman system of administration and against the manner in which certain persons manipulate these methods, then I cannot and will not deny it. [What was not yet understood in some countries was the way public opinion was formed in Holland.] What, in other countries, is thought and talked about privately, is printed with us. It would be a great mistake to think that, if elsewhere certain opinions and ideas are not allowed to emerge to the surface, the problems do not exist there. . . . I know one country where people are restricted to the writing of anonymous letters to foreign Cardinals who are expected to have some understanding and feeling for the problem (of celibacy). I have no wish to say whether the first method is preferable to the second. But on no account should one say that the problem does not exist simply because nobody has or can have the courage to express himself on such a point in public.'

It should be mentioned that *L'Osservatore Romano* not only printed a statement which said emphatically that the encyclical was not aimed at any particular country, but it also printed Alfrink's address—except, of course, the quotation which began with 'I know one country . . .'—that was obviously too much to swallow!

Some Dutch reactions to the results of Vatican II may have

been too negative and too pessimistic, and people may have pointed too exclusively to what the Council had *not* achieved and not enough to the genuine achievements and their significance for both the present and the future. It is certain that immediately after the Council there was a general mood of disillusionment. Gradually people began to understand that in some ways the harvest was rich and the hope was growing that, in the words of the beloved Bishop Bekkers, 'the Council will never end', in other words, that the Council had stimulated a fruitful examination of conscience in various provinces of the Church, roused and put life into the people, and encouraged them to continue the work generously for the future of both Church and world.

To sum up I quote Professor Schillebeeckx who has said so well what the Council did to those Dutch Catholics:

'The paradox of this Vatican II seems to me that the principles of renewal expressed there will soon make the Council look out of date. . . . This seems a reproach, but is in fact, it seems to me, the highest praise one can give to this Council: it has set the Church going, detached it from the age of Constantine in which the Church has lived for fifteen centuries. Obviously, when a horse starts to gallop it may bolt. But it is also typical of this Council that it has produced the will to break with what observers have called "the ministry of fear" which was alive in the Catholic Church in the past and still is: the exercise of authority by fear instead of love.'

4 . EVERYONE'S BISHOP

Nico van Hees

'I am glad to be alive now because of the tremendous opportunities offered by our age to get away from a sugar-coated Christianity, if I may use this contradictory expression, and to build a Christianity that has character and personality. These opportunities are the specific blessing and grace of our time.'

The man who spoke these words died on 9 May 1966. He was fifty-nine and bishop of the diocese of 's Hertogenbosch in the southern half of Holland—Wilhelmus Bekkers.

When the news of his death came through, the conservative non-Catholic paper, *De Nieuwe Rotterdamse Courant*, wrote:

'When Pope John died this paper said that the "smiling Pope" was one of the best public relations officers of the Roman Catholic Church. We may say the same with regard to Bishop Bekkers. He was much more than Bishop of 's Hertogenbosch; he was a familiar figure in many Dutch homes, whether these homes had a crucifix on the wall or not.'

The non-Catholic liberal paper, *Algemeen Dagblad*, said that:

'Bishop Bekkers owed his popularity largely to the way in which he filled the gap which had arisen in the course of the centuries between the ordinary faithful and the hierarchy. The discussion groups which he set going in his diocese during the Council put him in direct contact with the people themselves. And so he came to know thoroughly the real problems of ordinary church-going folk, problems which used to reach a bishop mainly after having been passed through the sieve of a hierarchical administration.'

The Protestant paper, *Trouw*, wrote in a similar vain:

'Now we have lost Monsignor W. Bekkers, bishop of 's Hertogenbosch. By "we" I mean the great community of all Dutch Christians of whatever denomination, who pray and work for the unity of Christ's Church. . . . He was a bishop

63

with a vision, a vision which embraced the Church of the
future. It is not to be wondered that we feel the loss of this
dynamic personality. Had he lived longer, he could have
achieved so much for all of us. Humanly speaking, he could
have brought us much closer to a united Church.'

The organ of the socialist party, *Het Vrije Volk*, remarked the
day after his death:

'The news of Bishop Bekkers' death will be a shock for many
Dutchmen outside Roman Catholic circles. Nobody can
remember any man vested with episcopal authority who
became so popular and was so warmly appreciated by both
Christians and non-Christians. . . . His character was such that
he had practically no fear of publicity; he sincerely wanted to
meet the world outside the Church. He thought that the
Catholic Church might as well abandon all hope if she were not
prepared to listen to others.'

And the Socialist weekly, *Vrij Nederland*, wrote:

'The Catholic Church had in him a representative who restored
the world's confidence in the aims of Christianity, who made
the faith again something to be respected and disengaged it
from the sly methods and lust for power practised in the name
of the Lord.'

Of the Catholic papers, the conservative *De Tijd* observed;

'He was a pioneer and leader of international stature.'

And the progressive *Volkskrant*:

'Perhaps Bishop Bekkers' early death was his last exhortation
to find the way oneself, to dare accept one's own responsibility,
not to believe that docility is the virtue *par excellence*.'

Wilhelmus Marinus Bekkers was born on 20 April 1908, at St
Oedenrode, an agricultural community in the mainly Catholic
province of Brabant in the South of Holland, as the eldest of
thirteen children. His father was a peasant.

After his education for the priesthood he began his work, in
1933, as a young curate in a labourers' parish in 's Hertogenbosch.

In 1939 he became rector of a boys' boarding school in the
industrial town of Eindhoven but was at the same time

commissioned to make way for Catholic action in the diocese, as
Pius XII had urged so strongly.

In 1942 he was appointed rector of a convent of contemplative
nuns in Den Bosch (Dutch abbreviation of 's Hertogenbosch),
director of the diocesan Catholic action and ecclesiastical assistant
to the agricultural union. In this last capacity he travelled up and
down the diocese. For seven years an important part of his work
consisted of conducting 'marriage-weeks', an activity which
reached its peak during the war. He was able to concentrate on this
because during the German occupation any organizational life
among farmers and industrial labourers was suppressed. In this
personal contact with thousands of married couples he gained the
experience which bore fruit later when he became known as the
'bishop of the married couples'.

During this period he was seriously injured in a car accident. It
was rumoured that he had died but the village doctor persevered
and at last he recovered.

In 1946 he shared in the direction of the organization for
'family care'. At this time he engaged in journalism as director
and editor of the diocesan weekly magazine. In 1948 he was made
adviser to the diocesan 'Catholic workers' movement'. Here he
became familiar with the special labour problems of a Brabant
that was rapidly becoming industrialized. He became an enthusiastic supporter of the industrial apostolate which he helped to
start and which now covers the whole diocese.

In 1956 he was made parish priest of the popular parish of
Tilburg, a centre of the textile industry, but this was only for a
few months because that same year he was appointed coadjutor
to Bishop Mutsaerts, with the right of succession. As his motto he
chose *Caritas pro armis* which he himself translated as 'Love for a
weapon'.

In 1960 Bishop Mutsaerts retired and thus Bishop Bekkers
became the sixth resident bishop of Den Bosch since the
restoration of the Dutch hierarchy in 1853. Within six years he
had become a national figure greatly loved by both Catholics and
non-Catholics.

In the beginning of 1961 he appeared in a topical magazine

c

programme on television and his influence began to extend itself beyond the boundaries of his diocese. He did for Dutch Catholicism what Pope John did in a few years for the world Church. He broke through the isolation in which the Dutch Church had lived throughout most of its history. He began by attempting to eliminate that deeply rooted mutual suspicion with which Dutch Catholics and non-Catholics regarded each other. For the first time non-Catholics encountered a prelate on equal grounds, simply as a normal fellow-citizen. The bishop of the neighbouring diocese of Breda, Bishop de Vet, who also died young (26 March 1967), wrote: 'We can only be sad at the passing of Bishop Bekkers, our good friend, neighbour and colleague.... He was a bishop whose influence extended far beyond the boundaries of his own diocese. He rendered innumerable services to the Dutch Church.'

Within a few years Bishop Bekkers became the hierarchical representative of the renewal movement, the *aggiornamento*, of the Dutch Province. His name spread over the whole world. On 18 May 1966 the American magazine *Time* devoted an article to him. The *New York Times* of 17 January wrote:

'The Dutch are ahead of the flock in the drive launched by Pope John XXIII to revitalize the Roman Catholic Church and give the faith new meaning in the modern world. They have acted faster and gone further in Pope John's *aggiornamento* than almost anyone else and some of their ideas question doctrine in a basic way. Priests, theologians and laymen say that the ferment has been good for the Church, that Dutch Catholics—about forty percent of the population of twelve million—are committed, that what is going on is giving the church meaning for younger people. ... Dutch Catholics have taken their cue from the late Bishop Willem Bekkers, much revered here for his work in the new theology, who once said on television that birth control was a matter of individual conscience. Dutch theologians have been prominent among those who have tried to lift the question out of the sphere of ecclesiastical legislation and treat it primarily as a human problem of spiritual, mental and physical welfare.'

After all that has been said here about Bishop Bekkers one might expect his personality to have been strikingly original and his disposition and character to have predestined him to lead and shape the renewal movement in Holland. But then he would not have fitted into the traditional patterns of the Dutch faithful who practised loyalty and docility towards the hierarchy and considered these the highest virtues. For generations Dutch Catholics had been exemplary in maintaining what they had inherited from their ancestors. In their isolation they had clung without criticism to the rules laid down by Rome for the world Church. Every papal encyclical was so to speak accepted as an infallible statement. Without ever asking whether what such a statement contained applied to the situation in Holland, they always got down at once to the immediate execution of the papal directives.

Thus, in the thirties, the Dutch bishops concentrated their efforts on Catholic action, which was so dear to the heart of Pius XII, and which made sense in Italy and other countries where there was no existing framework of Catholic action. But in Holland, long before the days of Pius XII, religious and social life had been organized along the lines of the social encyclicals of earlier popes, which had simply been shelved in various other countries.

It was a relief when the obedient and docile priests and layfolk of Holland came to the conclusion, after many fruitless efforts to find new applications for Catholic action, that their own way of organizing it, which they had worked out over so many years, was in fact Catholic action in the full sense of the term. They realized that the new Catholic action added nothing to what already existed. Bishop Bekkers was simply one of those who were wholly dedicated to the application of what pope and bishops had been asking for.

He grew up in an ordinary peasant family in Sint Oedenrode. Country people are naturally inclined to conservatism, and Bishop Bekkers lived all his life by the traditional pattern of the Christian peasant which his father had set him. After his death, Professor Schillebeeckx, who had come to know him very well during the Council, said:

'Bishop Bekkers could assimilate apparent contradictions with

uncomplicated ease. Princely postures were totally foreign to
him, but when he pontificated with mitre and crozier he could,
at the consecration of a church, with sweeping gestures of
archaic exuberance drive out all the devils with the holy water
sprinkler and he did this with a grim earnestness as if these
devils would only flee as far as his gesture could reach. Such
moments were for him the few occasions when he could really
pontificate because these moments could still contain something of the primitive human force from a peasant past in
a mighty liturgical gesture. He performed his liturgical gestures
with the visible satisfaction of the authentic *homo ludens*, man
at play.'

Till the very end Bekkers felt himself a son of the soil. Most
seminarians of peasant origin gradually grow away from the life
of their parents. They lose that attraction for fields, nature,
animals and growing crops. As a student Bekkers maintained his
contact with farm life. When he went home he made the round of
the fields with his father. He inspected the crops and the animals.
When he arrived, one of the first things he did was to visit the
sheds where the cattle were. Four of his brothers started their
own farm. Even as a fully occupied bishop he knew exactly how
things were with each of them. Till shortly before his death he
visited his parents' farm almost every week, riding his favourite
horse through the countryside.

Bekkers was in no sense a 'world-citizen'. He hated travelling
and was not really at home in the provincial town of Den Bosch
where his see was. He really loved the old familiar life on the land.
Although he worked so hard to update the ecclesiastical rules
for marriage and had such understanding for the problems
of modern marriage, he personally preferred the large family. He
himself was one of thirteen children. He was happiest in the
family circle with its old familiar pattern of life. And this pattern
included children, many children.

He was quite happy at the seminaries, both minor and major,
where he studied, and where he lived in an environment which
was hardly progressive or anxiously looking for new ways. In
those educational establishments there was neither a genuine
academic atmosphere nor a scientific climate of opinion. The

professors used to read from antiquated Latin textbooks of philosophy and theology, and the student learned these books by heart. Nobody felt the need for discussion or for what we now call 'free expression of opinion'. Even the professors had no opinions of their own.

The main rule of the minor seminary was: 'If you do as all the others do you are all right.' Anybody who was 'different' was considered an eccentric and was suspect. Walking along with the rest was the soul of good order. And this applied to leisure as well as to study. The mentality was that of the flat country of Brabant.

It was not very different in the major seminary. There the same line was pursued. All students had the same little rooms. Nobody was allowed to be different—in any field. This also held for the studies. Marks for work were never made known. The manner of studying, the use of one's time and the choice of reading had to be as uniform as possible.

Although the professors obviously encouraged diligence in study, they disapproved of students reading outside the usual textbooks. They frequently repeated the adage: *Timeo virum unius libri* (I fear the man who knows one book really well). It never dawned upon them that nothing is more dangerous than the man who is limited to one opinion. Everything was directed towards the formation of men whose thoughts were uniform. All originality was resisted. As a seminarian Bekkers put up with all this cheerfully. He had reasonable ability but no particular gifts; he was in no sense a scholar. He never thought of acting on his own initiative. At the seminary he was liked, and fitted perfectly into the established framework. He took part in everything, social life, sport and leisure. This was considered virtuous and proper and was the rather lifeless and colourless ideal presented to the future priest. And Bekkers believed in it.

This atmosphere continued after ordination. Then, too, one did what all the others did. Priests faithfully met at the regular clerical social evenings. That was the best proof that one was a good priest. In those years it did not occur to anyone that a man could have ideas of his own and that such ideas should be aired. It is a fact that Bekkers continued to live in this climate of opinion till after 1953. Therefore if at a later date one still finds his signature on regulations concerning 'dancing', 'fashions', disapproval of socialist trade unions and the socialist party, one should refrain from seeing in this the expression of his *own personal* conservative judgement. He simply regarded it as normal to support the judgement of others who signed such regulations. He did it because it seemed the normal thing to do.

All this must be seen against the background of what was generally accepted. That was what people wanted, that was safe. People did not ask for anything else. In their hearts people remained supicious of every thought that was original or out of the normal run.

Yet, to be fair, it must be said that within the circle of intellectually select clergy there was a genuine potential for originality. This is the reason for the sudden breakthrough during the period (1953-60) which preceded the years when Bekkers was bishop. At that time the intelligent clergy began to see that to leave everything uncritically as it had always been was really rather abnormal. Science had developed and the modern world had taken great strides forward while the life of the Church dragged along behind. This would no longer do.

The clergy and educated laity seized the opportunity to do something about it themselves, to think things out for themselves. As a priest Bekkers did not belong to the group that initiated the change, but he was open to its influence. He had faced the social problems of peasants and industrial workers and the post-war problems of married life.

Years later, in 1961, when he had already been bishop for five years, he spoke about marriage to one of his closer priest friends. He was in France on one of his rare journeys abroad when the car broke down. The travellers walked about outside the town of Limoges and saw in the distance the great new blocks of flats. His friend wrote:

'There we stood talking very seriously. We talked about the people who lived there, who did not go to Church on Sunday, did not fulfil their "duties", paid no attention to their Easter obligations etc., and are thus currently considered bad Catholics. What kind of contact do the people of the tenth floor now have

with the Church? What have we left to say to this kind of
people? We then talked about the "marriage weeks" during the
war and I felt that really the bishop welcomed the new age as a
liberation. He was very concerned about the problems of
marriage. He hoped to have an opportunity to find a new, radically different, solution. Before 1958 it would not have dawned
on him to diverge from what was generally accepted.'

Up till 1958 most of us still lived by the classical pattern: the
doctrine we preach is centuries old and is founded on infallible
pronouncements of general councils. That was beyond question.
On social problems, the encyclical *Quadragesimo Anno* and the
principle of subsidiarity laid down the directives. All these things
were seen as eternal truths, and it had not penetrated that such
matters needed further study. The encyclical was the only manual,
the unchangeable heritage of the faith, it could not be touched.

A very old and wise priest of the diocese of Den Bosch told me
once:

'When we penetrate into that really ecclesiastical environment
of the clergy and the clerical-minded, we have to start with the
fact that they had grown up in a milieu that was not wholly
normal. They had atrophied. Then things opened up, and for
the majority this happened very suddenly. But almost all felt
it as a kind of relief. They started to throw off things they had
always regarded as part of themselves. The evolution of ordinary people in society cannot be compared with the development of an art form or a cultural pattern. This was something
different.'

For himself, in his own devotional and spiritual life, Bekkers
did not feel the need for this new development. He was not conscious of any conflict between his peasant background and his
clerical formation. At first he saw the social problem in the light
of the papal documents. He was no theoretician. He would never
support modern thought as a system. But he could pick out very
cleverly and intelligently what he needed for the people. During
his last years his encounters with modern thought became increasingly fruitful.

Bekkers' appointment as bishop in 1960 coincided with the
turn of the tide, under the influence of Pope John, in his diocese.

The 'forward' thinkers of his diocese waited anxiously to see
whether the bishop would take the right line. It soon became clear
that he would and the intelligentsia backed him up. But it would
be wrong to conclude that he allowed himself to be taken in tow.
In fact, it happened the other way round. In listening to his advisers he allowed them hitherto unknown freedom in the expression of their ideas. Then Bekkers proceeded to adapt these ideas
to pastoral practice.

After his death the Protestant theologian G. T. Rothuizen
wrote:

> 'Where the most brilliant Catholic theologians in Holland
> failed, the bishop succeeded through the genuine simplicity
> with which he managed to move the heart of both Church and
> people.'

His successor, Bishop Bluyssen, said:

> 'He knew how to hit a bull's eye; and though the accent falls
> here on the "bull's eye" as much as on the shooting, he loved
> shooting and did it well and often. One can also put it like this:
> he had a heart and he had guts.'

Although himself no professional theologian, Bekkers inspired
theological thought. The Jesuit Jan van Kilsdonk, well-known in
Holland, wrote:

> 'Did Bekkers strike one as a gifted theologian? No. Even in
> Holland there are bishops who know more about theology than
> he did. Was he a brilliant speaker? Not really. Something
> stirred in him that was much deeper than all this. He had a
> quality of spiritual freedom which seemed to us unique.'

Schillebeeckx said in a memorial address to university professors
and students:

> 'Expressions such as "conservative" and "progressive" did not
> belong to his vocabulary: these labels were too academic for
> him. His language only knew the contrast between genuine or
> not genuine, true to life or not true to life. . . . Human life, from
> day to day, touched by God's grace, was his *locus theologicus,*
> the point from which his theology started, the source of his
> faith, his sermons, his prayer and the optimism of his faith. . . .
> If Bishop Bekkers created a new image of the bishop, an
> image which made the episcopal function acceptable even for

non-episcopalian and Protestant Christians and non-believers, it is because he had the courage never to hide himself behind the function. Such courage can indeed "compromise" a functionary, whatever his function, and Bekkers was aware of that. But one who refuses to run for cover becomes in the end invulnerable, even in suffering and sorrow, and people will worship him. . . . That was the reason why in critical circles such as the student circles of the universities of Leiden, Louvain, Amsterdam, Ghent, Delft, Rotterdam and Tilburg, people flocked to his guest lectures; a non-academician was enthusiastically applauded by academicians.'

Such statements might create the impression that the 'scholars' tried, after Bekkers' death, to surround his head with an artificial academic halo. It was the non-academic people, believers or non-believers, who must be credited with having discovered Bekkers as an exceptional man before the academic world.

There have been relatively few men in authority who have stimulated a renewal in theology. Authority generally prefers the brake to the spur. Bekkers belonged to that rare type that refuses to take the line of 'wait-and-see'. He gathered powerful forces around himself in order to give a lead at their head, covering them with his authority and the security of his episcopal status. In his diocese thinkers could breathe and speak freely.

In the first pastoral letter he wrote after the resignation of his predecessor, Bekkers outlined his plans for the future. He would concern himself specially with marriage, the family, the young people, ecumenism and pleasant co-operation with his priests. During the few years after 1960 he laboured indefatigably at these concerns. He won the hearts of millions of Dutchmen through his regular television appearances in which he would tackle burning topics with great frankness. Even non-Catholics used to speak of 'our' bishop. One Saturday night shortly before his death, as he sat working in his study, there was a ring at the door. A bus-load of Protestants from southern Holland stood outside asking whether they might shake hands with the television bishop. Bekkers went out in his slippers, shook hands with each of them and gave them a blessing.

Bekkers' ecumenism went far beyond friendliness and understanding. His right-hand man, Monsignor Rooyackers, told me:
'He encouraged anything that led in the direction of ecumenism
with extraordinary generosity. If a Protestant pastor rang him
up, he always had time, however full his agenda may have
been. He very frequently visited the Protestant pastor van den
Akker (the Reformed pastor of mainly Catholic Den Bosch) to
ask his opinion. He saw unity as practically existing already. At
any meeting or celebration a pastor always received a special
welcome. He always wanted to go as far as possible although he
recognized that there were still many difficulties.'

Pastor van den Akker founded the Den Bosch discussion
group where priests and pastors met regularly. Bekkers was
keenly interested. When the discussion went over his head, he
often intervened: 'Now put it in such a way that a simple bishop
can also understand it.' Pastor van den Akker says:

'We reached the important conclusion that in all outward-going
activities we should do together everything we could do
together, and do it to the limit. The Advent meetings of
Catholics and Protestants in the Cathedral of St John created
a great stir. This took place for the first time in 1960. We felt
the need to hold Advent services for both believers and non-
believers. At such a meeting the burgomaster (mayor) read the
gospel of Christmas, the pastor or bishop gave an address and
there was much singing together.'

The preparation for the Council prompted Bekkers to intensify
his contact with the Reformed Churches. With them he went into
a thorough discussion of the schema on ecumenism. According to
van den Akker,

'He gradually got a clear view of the "churchness" of non-
Catholic Christians. He saw there an evangelic quality. When
we get to know each other better and suspicion is put
aside, ecumenism becomes a constantly growing process of
recognition.'

Bekkers considerably improved the pastoral climate which
surrounded the question of mixed marriages. Once he let a
Catholic girl go to Protestant catechism instructions because
she felt she had to know more about the Protestant faith with

which she was ill-acquainted. Bekkers thought it important for Catholics to test their own beliefs in dialogue with non-Catholics. Ecumenism for him was not a matter of professionalism. It had to be pursued in the community. Once the socialist paper *Het Vrije Volk* wrote:

'The sheep of the Catholic flock were occasionally terrified at all the topsy-turvy manoeuvres of which, according to them, Den Bosch was guilty. A curate told us once that in his opinion the bishop had set a dangerous course. And he was not alone. ... When the bishop frankly suggested that in some ways the Reformers had developed the truth further than the Catholics, some called him a modern Luther. If Bekkers observed that the ecumenical movement was not a return of the others to Catholicism but an adventure common to all, his Catholic critics called him vague.'

The Protestant Johan Winkler wrote:

'I don't think I am the only Protestant who called him "my Bishop", because we looked on him like that, not because we wanted to harness him in one way or another to our own particular band-wagon, nor because we pretended to have discovered a kind of Protestant-minded Catholic in him, but simply because in some admirable way, and without being aware of it himself, he managed to exercise his episcopal authority also over us. There was here something like a mysterious breakthrough. The bishop of Den Bosch was unexpectedly and subconsciously "recognized" by more and more Protestants. Here one could, even though one had never met him personally, speak of an ecumenical "encounter", more direct and valuable than many a dogmatic discussion with which professional theologians hope to serve the cause of ecumenism.'

Bekkers himself said:

'Formerly ecumenism consisted only of the question how the return to Rome could be brought about. This question is now out of date. ... Many a Catholic has discovered to his amazement that there are advances which can be made by the Catholic Church as well as by the others.'

J. B. T. Spaan wrote in a pamphlet after Bekkers' death:

'Bishop Bekkers was a man who had seen a vision, the vision of one Christian Church. What would it look like? He did not know and did not pretend to know, but he saw a glimmer of it in a perhaps distant future and steered in that direction. He thought that the Roman Catholic Church, and all the Churches that strive after unity, are one people on the way and that on this way they had to talk together.'
But Bekkers went further. Once he said in an interview:
'We shall have to recognize the value of non-Christian religions and to develop the Christian values present in them by taking the Church there. And what the encyclicals have to say, for instance, will have to fit in with that. But here, too, it is a matter of first looking for the other by trying to get to know him. For we with our Western culture have still no idea of the content of the non-Christian religions of other parts of the world and the values of these religions.'

Being a bishop, Bekkers took part in the Council. He was not there for pleasure. Far from home in a strange city this man of the soil did not feel at ease. By nature keen on as much contact as possible with his fellow man, he often felt isolated in Rome because he had no foreign languages.
As a great lover of football this Council father enjoyed most the great international matches played in the Roman stadium. Professor Heiko Oberman, of the theological faculty of Harvard, Massachusetts, a Dutchman by birth and an observer at the Council, got to know Bekkers in the stadium at such a match. 'After the match,' he said, 'we had a very serious discussion about . . . the best beer in the world.'
Someone who takes this question of the Church in the world seriously might well ask what a non-Catholic theologian saw in Bekkers. Oberman said:
'Bekkers was not a man of profound knowledge but he had a sense of theological niceties. In a very short time he could draw you out on many things and a week later he seemed to have assimilated the lot. I was on the point of taking him to America because I felt that he had a way of putting things with which he could set all kinds of ideas moving in the United States. I

believe that he would have had an enormous influence on
ordinary people. Bekkers was immediately enthusiastic about
the idea. He had already begun to learn English. Three
weeks before he died he wrote to me: "I am not sure whether I
shall make it in March." And I believe that Church historians
will later on agree that Bekkers was on the right path. It is a
blessing that today men like Bekkers can become a bishop. We
could do with many more men like Bekkers in Holland before
reaching the danger point.'

The great significance of Bekkers for the Council was that in
Rome he sparked off the dialogue among the bishops. Before the
bishops went to Rome, they received the draft texts for the
conciliar schemas. Professor Schillebeeckx still remembers clearly
that a first reading of these schemas made Bekkers wonder
whether a general Council was really necessary if the bishops had
nothing to do but approve these texts which were so out of
touch with life. So Bekkers went into action with his secretariat
and some theologians. The texts were critically examined and
annotated. They were so to say re-written according to modern
theological opinion. In this state the revised schemas were translated into Latin, English and French, because Bekkers intended
that these texts should be put into the hands of the Council
Fathers.

When Bekkers arrived in Rome with his staff for the first
session, all was ready. Schillebeeckx says:

'The bishops from all over the world had hardly arrived for the
first time in Rome, on 11 October 1962, when over them and
their retinues washed four thousand dossiers containing constructive or negative criticisms of the preliminary schemas,
which Bekkers called "alien to man and to the world". Many
foreigners with inside knowledge agree that this action
undoubtedly influenced the spirit of the first session and its
breakthrough. . . . After a month other bishops were copying
Bekkers' initiative. . . . With this Bekkers felt that he had made
his contribution to the Council. He left the further development of it to the growing two-thirds majority among the
Council Fathers.'

Bekkers' main disability during the Council was his lack of languages. This limited his activity. And yet, at the place where the Dutch bishops were lodged, it was Bekkers who was most in demand and received most telephone calls. The press, too, paid a great deal of attention to him. Once he was rung up by Cardinal Ottaviani and asked to come along. Bekkers felt ill at ease and feared that the Prefect of the Holy Office was going to reprimand him. The Cardinal asked him, among other things, why it was that so many priests in his diocese left the priesthood. Bekkers explained to the Cardinal that he had in his diocese more than eight hundred active priests and several hundred religious, and that the percentage of those who fell out was very small. Ottaviani realized that he had yet again been spitefully misinformed. Bekkers used the occasion and the relaxed atmosphere to recommend that the marriages of two former priests, whose cases had been dragging on for years, should be sanctioned. (Consent was given in these cases shortly afterwards.) He had come to this meeting with Ottaviani with a heavy heart, but he left a happy man, and later on he often referred to this successful encounter.

At the same time as the sessions in Rome, the so-called 'pastoral discussions' were proceeding in Bekkers' own diocese. There were thousands of these groups, consisting of laity, clergy (regular and secular), as well as non-Catholics, who exchanged their reactions to a given topic. The results were collected and brought to the notice of the whole diocese.

These discussions attracted an increasing number of participants. The first topic was confession, the second the Eucharist and during the last year of the Council, 1965, the important schema XIII on the Church and the world. More than twenty thousand people took part. The last series of discussions was started off by the Bishop himself, who came over from Rome for the purpose. He said:

'As I have just assisted at the conciliar discussion on schema XIII I must say that many of the Fathers still think of the "Church *in* the world" as the "Church *over against* the world". For many Fathers "world" is a collective name for evil, hostility

to God, paganism. .... Thank heavens, it is the opinion of a
minority.'

He went on:

'The pastoral discussion this year will not be a matter of teaching the laity but of learning from the laity. It is the priest who
must become the "listening" Church, the layman the "speaking"
Church. .... The opinion of faithful Catholics is obviously important. But perhaps the opinion of so-called "fringe" Catholics
is equally important, I mean the opinion of people who are said
to practise little or not at all. You may think what you like of
these people but there are among them men who live more
sincerely and genuinely than those church-goers who refuse to
stake their "all risks" insurance, in other words, who are only
motivated by "duty" and "sin". The participation of fringe-
Catholics is also important because they encounter and belong
to the society where God is not tolerated, is not "present" without prejudice, and because they may help us to understand
through their experience what kind of a world and what kind of
ideas about the Church are the cause of the decline. .... A
Church that is uniform all over the world will die.'

While we are dealing with the way in which Bekkers personi-
fied the renewal in the Church of Holland, we must naturally
mention the question of marriage, so fiercely discussed in Holland
in recent years. When Bekkers had finished the address I have
quoted from at the municipal theatre of Tilburg, the textile centre
of Brabant, he walked into the foyer where many people were
having a cup of tea. Children were all over the floor. He picked
up one of the toddlers, and turned laughing to the bystanders and
said: 'Isn't it a pity, this celibacy.'

During the brief years of his pontificate Bekkers was known
throughout the country as 'the bishop of the married couples'.

Marriage was the subject that preoccupied him for a large part
of his life. For so far as we can retrace these years, we get
the impression that as a priest Bekkers always took the papal
directives, set out in *Casti Connubii,* as the fixed starting-point
for his instructions given to married or engaged couples, but
was always very elastic when people came to him with their
actual difficulties. So he began to sense that the old legalistic

attitude was no use to these people and he began to see in marital
love itself the starting-point and the source for guidance.

When, many years later, he discussed marriage with the priests
of his diocese as auxiliary bishop, we notice that he had
developed his position significantly. He did not produce revolutionary ideas. But, in contrast with many of his colleagues and
some moral theologians, he no longer defended the Church
against people. He got, so to speak, into the skin of those who
were married. Starting from their urgent distress and their
hankering after a personal and unoppressive marital love, he
searched with them for a deliverance from an intolerable burden
which, as he saw it, was imposed by the 'absolutism' of the
Church's law on all questions of marriage.

In 1957 and 1958 he mentioned these problems to his priests.
He introduced the subject in a way which prompted discussion.
He said:

'Am I going too far when I maintain that not only do many
married couples live in unrest and uncertainty but that we,
priests, suffer from the same uncertainty? I have the idea that
we have inherited the attempt to imprison the beauty and
sanctity of marriage in its definition as "the right to each other's
body for procreation". The straight and consistent application
of this definition makes the priest rigid and alienated in such a
way that he himself starts looking for ways of correcting it. He
is determined to help people, he finds that he must put some
water into the wine. But this is often done with a secretly heavy
conscience because he feels that he is really moving on to the
slippery slope of laxity and, *faute de mieux*, he feels that he
has to draw the line somewhere, at random and in individual
cases. . . . And now we see—and is this not the heart of the
matter?—that both laity and priests are incapable of giving sex
its place in marriage and in the totality of life, not even in the
totality of well-intentioned Christian life. So why are we surprised when we are forced to admit that it is our inability to
consider the sexual problems of marriage and family life within
the context of life as a whole that is one of the main sources of
leakage in our time? And can we ever succeed in overcoming
this inability as long as we shove religion, prayer, humility,

justice, charity into one room but always have to reserve a separate room for chastity? Even so, many things have already escaped from that room. Previously, that is where we kept dancing, mixed recreation, fashions, films, more broadminded conventions for boys and girls. It seems to me urgent that we really think about this, do not fight shy of honest discussion, reminding ourselves that while we may call ourselves the preservers of the sacrament we are not entitled to behave like commanding officers. We must be companions to all men, we must be people who listen and can fit in. The notion that we are "searchers" may help to eliminate innumerable rigid hardships and ready-made judgements. We may call ourselves guides for people who do not have to fall in with us but with whom it is rather up to us to fit in. This demands that we know the nature of married life, with its social and cultural conditions. . . . This does not mean that the moral textbook has become superfluous. But surely it means that to limit oneself to a textbook will result in a totally inadequate judgement.'

The reader will realize that in this instruction Bekkers is still in the preliminary stages of the modern problem of marriage. Here he is still mainly preoccupied with relieving the pressure of sin which moral theology imposed on sex in its various expressions.

He is well aware that human love and sex are connected, and not, like holiness and sinfulness, at opposite ends of the pole. He wishes to set at rest the minds of those whose consciences are caught in this apparent contradiction. But even then, at the end of the 1950s, he gave evidence of an open mind on the whole issue. Among other things he asked his priests: 'Can we accept that sexual love belongs to the rational order? And therefore that reason can regulate it?' Here he is clearly alluding to intelligent parenthood and birth control. And he continued:

'Do we recognize the possibility that there are two "styles" or "types" of marriage, of which I would call the first the "spontaneous" type ("take what God gives") and the second that of rational birth regulation, which is gaining ground slowly but surely? If this is so, should we not mention this in our marital instructions for those that are or will get married? The harmonious fulfilment of the many values of marriage is a necessity. The mutual adjustment of these values depends to a large extent on the partners, their potentiality, difficulties, disposition, the history of their lives, and so on. But do we in fact admit this? And do we then accept the consequences, such as the fact that one cannot sacrifice mutual love and care for existing children to children only biologically possible? Do we accept that all values must be preserved and that there is a "technique" of marriage? That our preaching and guidance must present marriage in its fulness, and not only or mainly as an institution for procreation? Do we understand that a one-sided emphasis on the correct norm of marital intercourse (as we always used to call it) can do grave damage? Do we accept fully the primacy of love?'

As a solution the bishop was still thinking mainly in terms of the rhythm method, but he adds:

'Can we then condemn the continuation throughout of ordinary and I mean "ordinary" manifestations of love, since the growth of love, including bodily love, is a necessity? How many priests are severe in their conversation and in discussion and will have nothing to do with "unchastity" and then forgive everything in the confessional? Is this not really playing hide-and-seek with ourselves?'

Here we have a young bishop discussing things with priests. In those years he was not yet concerned with a ready-made solution. 'It is a question of insight, and not of a quick judgement,' he said. He was still mainly concerned with the relieving of pressures put on people by the Church in sexual matters. During those years he encouraged the setting up of 'well-staffed and well-equipped family advice centres'. In the autumn of 1959 the World Council of Churches pronounced in favour of birth control in any form that was found effective. This gave a fresh impulse to the discussion in Catholic circles. Just before Bishop Bekkers took over from his predecessor, the marriage issue in its modern version had become more mature and more acute in Holland. As he prepared himself for the Council Bekkers gave this his special attention. In the meantime he had become a popular television personality. His television appearance on 21 March 1963 became a national event. He began the programme as follows:

'Much is being said and written today about birth control. Through the discoveries of science man is now able to control procreation. The distribution of births has now come within the scope of man's responsibility. One may even say that birth control—which is different from mere limitation of births—will be part of the normal and total function of marriage.' [Talking about marital love, he added] 'This marital love must permeate home life and demands to be expressed in the total bodily condition of man, from a simple look, the caress and the kiss to the union of the bodies. In this human living out of marriage, and therefore from this mutual love and responsibility for each other, for their fruitfulness and for their already formed family, the married partners—and they alone—can answer the question of what God's vocation and their task in life can mean in practice, how big their family should be, and how the children should be spaced out. That is a matter for their conscience with which no one is entitled to interfere. Every manner of birth control still has something unsatisfactory because it implies the danger that the right view of marriage may be impaired or mutual fidelity may be lost. . . . Whatever the progress of science, we must ask ourselves whether the principal thing is not the deepening of man's existence, of that personal existence which allows man to control procreation in such a manner that it fits in with the conception of marriage I have just outlined.'

On 17 June 1964 he returned to the matter of the formation of conscience and said on television:

'The reality of daily life, in which we live and which we call "our world", is as wide and as deep as the sea, and it cannot be indispensable, just as the sailor cannot sail without the guidance of sun and stars. But the manner of his sailing depends on the sea and the situation on board. This image suits our life perfectly, as we come across everyday situations which demand a personal decision by our own conscience. The most striking example is doubtless married life and family life. By and large one marriage looks like another. All are in the same boat, on the same vast sea with the same compass. But character, health, accommodation, income, the man-and-wife relationship, the parent-children relationship, age, and so on, all these values, and perhaps lack of values, determine the shape of this particular marriage and make it different from all the others. There are, of course, general norms, just as the sailor has his stars. Man and wife stand on the bridge, look at the stars, but also watch out for the iceberg, the coming storm, the calm waters, the final goal, the provision of food on board, the sick one who needs help. All this together may lead to the decision to change course, the right decision if taken in love, out of care for the various interests which must be protected in the concrete situation of this particular family,—the right decision if taken with "love as weapon" [Bekkers' motto] and therefore a truly conscientious decision, even if it concerns the number of children. There must be general norms such as total mutual generosity; love must of course be prepared to sacrifice, but in a particular, individual situation, stronger emphasis may be needed on the communion of love than on procreation, and the application of general norms will then depend on the personal conscientious decision . . . I have thought this: that it is not the fulfilment of the law which is the norm of love but that love is the norm for the fulfilment of the law. Inspired by that command of love given by the Lord, the conscience may and must deal with laws and norms. And thus, I thought, the conscientious man grows up, giving himself with the intention of making the best of life without pretending to have the monopoly of wisdom. The personal conscience, born of love, is not an emergency brake allowing man to stop when he likes; it is not a backdoor through which to escape; it is not the line of least resistance. If conscience gives love its opportunity and this love is necessary in order to be human in the true sense, it means that man can and must do much more than merely obey. If he wanted merely to obey it would be better, as Professor Madinier puts it so bluntly, if man had an instinct of obedience rather than a conscience. Only with the inspiration of love, the voice of his conscience and a personal commitment can man look God and his fellow man straight in the eye.'

The bishop returned to these thoughts on a subsequent

occasion before the camera. There were some who accused him of
innovation. Bekkers observed laconically at the end: 'Is all this so
modern and progressive? Then I would like to conclude with
this. Everything I have said was already said prophetically a
hundred years ago by the famous Cardinal Newman.'

The last important document on marriage left behind by
Bishop Bekkers is a conversation he had, shortly before his illness
in December 1965, with the president of the non-Catholic Dutch
Society for Sexual Reform. Originally neo-Malthusian in
character the society did much in the course of the years to bring
about a better understanding of sexual life and established many
consultation bureaux in Holland where married couples could
obtain information and, if they wanted them, contraceptives.
Until recently strict Catholics frowned upon this society. Even in
1958 Bekkers, when still auxiliary bishop, said, 'Without a
methodical approach all action against this society is futile;
without trained people we fight a losing battle.' In 1964 the
president sought an interview with Bekkers, which took place at
the bishop's home in Den Bosch, and clarified ideas on both
sides. A year later, just after the Council had finished, the Bishop
himself asked for another interview with the president and approved the publication of their whole conversation in a Dutch
paper. Here he said among other things:

'Where new concepts, based on the discoveries of science, are
changing our concept of life, then the Church must adapt herself to the times we live in and to our understanding of life. . . .
If our concepts of man, of sex and marriage are changing in a
rather radical way, then the kind of directives we issue must be
changed too. . . . To the learned moral theologians I would say:
I love to hear your scholarly formulations, but for me the moral
theology which arises from the ordinary people is equally important. . . . The Church has often looked down on the world
from supernatural heights. This is not very realistic. In such an
enormously important age as this we are saddled with the
reproach made to the Church that for too long she has been
dilatory in facing up to her responsibility. But I am now more
optimistic than a year ago.'

Five months later, at the bishop's funeral, prominent among the flowers was a wreath from the Society for Sexual Reform, and many of its members attended the service.

Bishop Bekkers was not a curator of a museum of ecclesiastical antiquities. There were bishops and priests who were disquieted by him. They felt that he went too fast with his ideas and that his presentation of them was rash. It is, however, curious that among the more simple people he was practically never misunderstood. This was because he had gradually shaken off the evil of a 'double' morality, that attempt to compromise between principles that are supposed to be unchangeable and the deviation from them imposed by practical life. The last words I took down from him on this subject were:

'I reproach our Church with something and I don't know whether this reproach holds good, although it still seems justified at present. It is that there is still an official teaching, based on the past and with hardly any changes; and yet we tell people: if, in conscience, you decide you may do otherwise, God will understand. We have therefore an official doctrine of principles and a practical rule for people who cannot apply them and who would be simply irresponsible if they did apply them. And when they do not apply those official principles but act according to their good intentions God will obviously understand and be merciful nevertheless. Thus you get a double morality, and I believe that we must never accept that.'

Bishop Bekkers is dead. Yet, already, as in the case of Pope John, we may say without exaggeration that his work can no longer be undone. The doors he has opened cannot be closed. Bekkers turned a Church that thought she had but to command, into a Church that listened, and changed a religious and ecclesiastical command into an invitation. The result was that the number of people who listened to him grew every day and that the more he himself learned to ask questions the more his authority increased, both inside and outside the Church.

5. GOD'S PEOPLE ON THE WAY

Joseph J. Poeisz

Brief description of the past

Dutch Catholicism cannot be properly understood by outsiders if the historical situation out of which it grew is not taken into account. Foremost among the authors who have tried to give a sociological interpretation of this situation is Walter Goddijn, who has explained it in terms of opposing sociological groupings: the minority and the dominant.[1]

To understand the characteristic features of Dutch Catholicism we must go back to the Reformation in the sixteenth century, when the Catholic sector of the population became dependent on the originally small group of Protestants who had acquired political power. The relationship of these two sectors of the population was marked by pronounced intolerance. In 1573, for instance, Catholics were forbidden to gather for public worship. After this date fresh limitations were constantly imposed. These measures went beyond religious or ecclesiastical activities. Catholics were excluded from all higher offices, were not allowed to have their own schools, nor to study at foreign universities. Gradually as they were discriminated against by their fellow-countrymen socially, economically, politically and ecclesiastically, their situation became that of a minority.

The minority situation of the Dutch Catholics lasted for some centuries. It was bound to leave its mark on the group. This became clear at the end of the eighteenth century when, after the constitutional equalization of all Dutchmen, the Catholics had to go through a long process of emancipation before equality in principle became equality in fact. The restoration of the hierarchy

[1] W. Goddijn, *Katholieke minderheid en protestantse dominant* (Assen, 1957). See also F. van Heek, *Het geboorteniveau van de nederlandse rooms-katholieken* (Leiden, 1954).

in 1853 provided an indispensable stimulus to this process. Because of the centuries-old oppression and discrimination, the Catholic sector was inadequately equipped to restore the social, economic and political balance.

During the period of emancipation Dutch Catholicism was marked by a strong feeling of solidarity. As a continuation of the past, this reflected that inner cohesion typical of a minority situation. At the same time it was a factor which encouraged collective effort to achieve full emancipation in the future. This factor affected all the elements of the group. A Catholic had Catholic friends, married a Catholic partner, joined a Catholic organization, had a Catholic education, and uniformly supported the Catholic hierarchy. The hierarchy, sure of this support, helped to pave the way for full emancipation. This is why the hierarchy could afford to be somewhat authoritarian, not only in Church matters, but also in social, economic and political affairs, thereby reinforcing the unity and typical features of the group. The image, then, of Dutch Catholicism as it entered upon the twentieth century was of a tightly organized group, with an authoritarian structure at the top and a very docile disposition.[1]

In *society* Catholics were strongly inclined to avoid contact with non-Catholics. There was a certain fear based on a social inferiority complex, a suspicion of the intentions of the others, and a sense of not being a match for the religiously better educated Protestant. Friends and acquaintances were limited to those of the same faith. This was particularly the case where marriage was concerned, since marriage with a non-Catholic was felt as something to be ashamed of.

Organizational life was also marked by denominational segregation.[2] Here the pattern of social organization is based on the difference in attitudes to life, which is very prominent in Holland. One has but to look at the fields in which this kind of segregation has taken place: trade unionism, political organization, radio, and later also television, the press, education, sport,

---

[1] For a summary of these studies, see J. J. Poeisz, 'Gruppenisolierung, Kirchlichkeit und Religiösität' in *Internationales Jahrbuch für Religionszsoiologie* (Cologne, 1965).

[2] J. P. Kruyt and W. Goddijn, 'Verzuiling en ontzuiling als sociologisch process', in *Drift en Koers* (Assen, 1962).

youth movements, culture, societies for recreational pursuits, etc.[1] This phenomenon can also be seen as the expression of the solidarity prevailing in each denomination's social organization. Until recently the hierarchy, and the Catholic political organizations, unions, educational organizations, press, radio and television spoke with one voice, forming a closely-knit whole, matched a similar exclusiveness on the part of Protestants by the socialists and the 'neutrals'.

Religious practice showed these same features in the emancipation period. A 'good Catholic' was not merely expected to be religious but also to support the social, economic and political activities of the group. He faithfully followed the directives for behaviour in Church and society laid down by the Church. He asked no questions but simply did what was expected of him. He had no specifically religious motives for his conduct. Normally his actions were motivated by an awareness that it was his duty to live in accordance with the Church's expectations.

Within the *hierarchical structure of the Church* there was no room for the laity. One did not expect criticism from 'below' and the 'voice of the people' was not heard. The loyalty of the faithful was sufficient guarantee for the punctual execution of the Church's regulations and this provided the hierarchy with the means to fulfil their task. The number of vocations was high and financial contributions were abundant.

But as the twentieth century proceeded, far-reaching changes made themselves felt in the Catholic sector of the population. Emancipation attained its ends and a new way of living in society emerged.[2]

The past is over

Emancipation developed in the nineteenth and twentieth centuries against a background of industrialization and urbanization of a once predominantly agrarian society. Political, economic and educational equality was begun in an agrarian community

[1] Cf. Centraal Bureau voor de Statistiek. Vrijetijdsbesteding in Nederland, vol. 6, *Verenigingsleven* (Zeist, 1957).

[2] H. and W. Goddijn, *De kerk van morgen* (Roermond, 1966).

and ended in an industrial, urban society. It was also the result
of changes in the social context in which Catholics lived and took
place at all levels.

Urban society is marked in a high degree by anonymity and
mobility. This obstructs the pattern of contacts between those of
the same faith. The development of friendships and acquaintances becomes much more dependent on casual meetings. Thus
the work environment assumes great significance.

In an urban society the emphasis falls on the highest possible
achievement. Every society, organization or institution strives
to achieve the highest possible quality of services or of pro-
ductivity. The fact that an organization consists of members of
the same faith usually contributes little to the quality of service
and achievement. In some cases it may even be an obstacle, as in
instances where the number of members falls below the level
required for a sound functioning of the organization. The
significance, therefore, of an organization based on an attitude
towards, or philosophy of, life becomes less important. Priority
is given to good education, a sound press, good political organization, whilst ideological schools, papers and political parties
occupy a secondary place. This finds expression in a process of
'de-segregation': firstly, because of the loss of propaganda value
of ideological organizations, and secondly, because of a diminution of solidarity within the segregated, denominational sector.
It is a common practice now for organizations to criticize, attack,
approve each other quite frankly according to the way each fulfils
its specific task. The same holds for the relationship of the organizations with the hierarchy.

Another characteristic of industrial urban society is the emphasis on personal responsibility for one's situation in life. This
society creates equal opportunities for its members to make their
own way in society. Each, however, can only rely on himself to
make use of these opportunities: each one's own effort is the key.
In religious practice this attitude finds expression in the demand
to be personally responsible for one's own way of practising one's
faith. Acting out of duty is increasingly replaced by acting on one's
personal interpretation of religious values. This means a shift in

the way religion is experienced. Traditionally religious practice was the fulfilment of duties in Church and society as prescribed by authority. In an urban society it is rather characterized by a man's personal religious interpretation of his situation in life. Each expresses his religious life in his own way, according to his conscience. It is in this way that each one is involved in religion. There is a certain pluriformity in the manner of this involvement.

The next feature is the democratic spreading of education to every layer of the population, Catholics included. The intellectual, social and ecclesiastical élite of the nineteenth century broadened considerably in outlook. This had wide repercussions on life in the Church. In place of the lofty ecclesiastical authority of the nineteenth century there arose in the course of the twentieth an élite of the laity, which gradually worked itself loose from ecclesiastical authority and steered the organizations along a course of their own choice. It was this group which later became the mouthpiece for the demand for renewal among Dutch Catholics, particularly the demand to be heard and to have a voice in many urgent questions that arose in the Dutch province. It was a demand for a more democratic organization of the hierarchical structure.

The minority situation of the Dutch Catholics and their striving after economic, political and educational equality was dominated by the isolation and solidarity of the group, by the submission of the individual to the group as a whole, and by the authoritarian nature of the hierarchy. The urban and industrial society, however, in which this equality has been achieved, demands openness and solidarity with society as a whole, a personal responsibility for one's own situation, a democratic relationship with authority. As emancipation reached its fulfilment, the requirements of the urban industrial society as a whole became more and more pressing on the Catholic sector. With the achievement of equality the motives for unity and solidarity broke down, and, curiously, the group which first defended unity now insisted with the same force on a maximum realization of the conditions demanded by urbanization and opposed those required in the earlier emancipation period.

The problems of the transition period

The Dutch province is now in a transition situation where the ballast of the emancipation period must be cast off and where people are looking for ways in which to meet modern society. The hierarchy is confronted with this situation at every level and is forced to take measures that hasten this adaptation. Here special mention must be made of the Catholic press, radio and television which have become the mouthpiece for the progressive part of the population and which constantly bring up problems that worry large groups of the population. In Holland we need a stoic calm to sort out, in these demands for renewal, what is genuine and what is not, what is adaptation and what is destruction. We are familiar with tradition and this has given us security. We have as yet no clear picture of what the renewal must look like. Life in the no man's land between old and new is exhausting. Small groups are disturbed and ask for an 'authoritative word' that will strengthen the old, while keen progressive groups ask for the 'word that will set us free' and that will make all problems vanish at the drop of a hat.

The problem for which we must find a solution is complex. It concerns Church life at every level: religious practice, organizations, the structures of the Church. This complexity has created a demand for an expert approach and thorough investigation. It has already given a strong impulse to religious sociology. In particular, the need to investigate the problem of decision taking is universally recognized, sometimes at the expense of 'basic research'. The Dutch Pastoral Council is the focal point of many of the demands for renewal made at present in Holland, and the giving of informed advice is an important part of its work. Some of this work is done on a voluntary basis. Some has been taken up by special and university institutes for sociological and psychological research.

I shall go on now to describe some areas where problems arise and place them as far as possible within their context.

From closed groupings to open ones

The tendency towards openness, which is present at all levels of the Catholic group in Holland, is marked by a high degree of tolerance towards what was formerly seen as a menace. And that included, by definition, the whole of society in so far as it was not Catholic nor regulated by Catholic laws, norms and directives. The lessons learned from this rigidity led to a determination to meet the other Churches. This explains the intense interest that Dutch Catholics are taking in the ecumenical movement. Those other Churches fully appreciated this change of front. It created an atmosphere of goodwill and mutual help, of trust and understanding. The degree of co-operation has, however, its limits, particularly where the existence of a group's own forms is called in question. Catholics are on the whole inclined to push this readiness further than Protestants. It is not impossible that a different emphasis in religious outlook plays a part in this. The Catholic Church in Holland has traditionally laid a good deal of emphasis on *group solidarity* and group entity; Protestant Christianity, within its community groupings, has laid much more stress on *living* and putting into practice its religious values.

This tendency towards openness penetrates every level of the life of the group, as may be seen in the following two examples.

1. *Mixed marriages and conversions.* In Holland mixed marriage is becoming more common, particularly in the urban agglomerations. In 1966, of all the marriages that involved a Catholic 15% were between a Catholic and non-Catholic. In towns with more than 100,000 inhabitants this figure reached 30%, while in the countryside it is much lower, only 2%.[1] This number has increased since 1957, particularly where the countryside has become urbanized.[2] Until recently mixed marriage was considered an attack on the unity of the group. On the clerical

---

[1] *Parochies in Nederland op 1 Januari 1966.* Memorandum n. 166 of the Katholiek Sociaal-Kerkelijk Instituut (Cath. Soc.–Rel. Inst.). (The Hague, 1966).

[2] P. A. van Leeuwen, "Kerkelijk gemengde huwelijken in Nederland, 1958–65," in *Katholiek Archief* (1966), n. 44.

side there was little tolerance of those who planned to marry a non-Catholic. On the whole the Catholic attitude was negative. A large majority (80%) of mixed marriages received no blessing from the Church.

Today the idea is growing that mixed marriage can no longer be approached in such a negative way. In urbanized areas it is certainly becoming more socially accepted and seen less as a danger to the life of the group. The objection to mixed marriages is diminishing and there is a more open attitude towards them. This development must be seen as an aspect of the general growth towards openness in the relations between the various denominations. This new attitude has also influenced the pastoral approach. An indication of this is that the discriminating regulations which used to accompany the Church's blessing of a mixed marriage have been withdrawn.[1] A difficult point remains the education of children of a mixed marriage. A small majority (55%) are of the opinion that the Church cannot insist on a Catholic education.[2]

A delicate point in the mutual relations between Catholics and Protestants is conversion. During the emancipation period 'conversion to the true faith' was the symbol of the strength of the group, a victory over competitors. A conversion in the opposite direction was 'apostasy'. This mentality has almost completely vanished. A non-Catholic today is 'received into the Catholic Church'. In 1965 1,700 Protestants and 1,500 non-Church members were thus 'received', which is a small number compared with the five million Catholics and seven million non-Catholics of Holland. The passage from one Church to another can be seen as a test of the growth towards openness. In general there is in Holland an attitude of loyalty on both sides. According to a recent investigation some 38% (taken from both Churches) would not object to their son or daughter changing their faith, whilst some 44% would regret it but accept it.[3] We know, however, that people's 'expressed opinion' usually shows more openness than is in fact the case. This became only too clear when a

[1] Cf. *Analecta* of the diocese of Rotterdam, 1966, pp. 3–4.
[2] The weekly paper *Margriet* (1966), n. 44.
[3] *Margriet* (1966), n. 42.

few years ago Princess Irene of the Royal House of Orange became a Catholic and married a Spanish prince. The stir this event created showed how very tender this growth towards openness still is. The 'Irene affair' brought out all the sensitivities that had for so long marked the tension between Catholic and Protestant.

2. *Social organizations.* The tendency towards co-operation with groups of another ideology and towards deconfessionalization is most pronounced in Catholic organizations. When solidarity ceased to be the motive for organization, there was no point in insisting on Catholic organizations. The main question became how far the actual organization contributed to the maximum achievement of the real purpose for which the organization existed specifically. The question became the more obvious as the diminution of the solidarity motive led to stagnancy or regression in the number of members. This made many organizations ask themselves whether they were really necessary. This was felt particularly with regard to the Catholic people's party (the political party with the relative majority in Holland), which within a few years began to realize that it was now being judged rather for what it achieved politically than for how Catholic it was. Here the process of 'desegregation' showed itself in sharp criticism from among its own members, and from the Catholic press, and also in the last general election when many Catholics no longer voted for their party. In 1963 the party had 29.1 percent of the total votes, in 1967 only 24.3 percent. The denominational bond has clearly become weaker and has brought to the fore the question of a revision of the party system as it exists now.

The growth towards co-operation in the field of organizations and institutions is far more apparent where new organizations with new functions and new provisions are called for. During the emancipation period the first concern was to maintain ideological differentiation even if this led to an organization pattern that was inadequate or of low quality. Today the first question is what needs must be filled and only then is the ideological differentiation examined when we bear in mind that this differentiation must in no way jeopardize the provisions made and that any separate organization must be able to function properly. This is how the matter of education must be looked at.

This new, open relationship between ideological organizations has also led during the last ten years to mutual consultation and co-operation. It is now usual, in such important fields as radio, television and trade unionism, to maintain close contact and to render each other a great number of services. The mentality which prevailed during the emancipation period has practically disappeared here.

Religious practice

The changes that have come over Catholic life in Holland have deeply affected religious practice. I have already pointed out that during the previous period a loyal and docile group of faithful lived scrupulously by ecclesiastical regulations, more than in any other country. When in 1966 for the first time Mass attendance was investigated in Holland it was proved that 64.4% of the Catholics actually fulfilled their Sunday obligation. This figure is perceptibly higher than the percentages established in earlier years in other countries of Western Europe. In 1961 *ICARES* brought out a report on Mass attendance in the 1950s in a number of countries. Although these figures are now out of date, they allow one to judge the relatively high figure in Holland. Compared with Holland's 64%, West Germany had 50, Austria about 35, Switzerland and Belgium about 50, France 30, and England, Scotland and Wales 40. Only Ireland showed a relatively higher percentage.[1]

This fairly high figure for Holland may be attributed to the peculiar situation during the emancipation period. A number of factors seem, however, to indicate that there will be a change here. We have very little factual information relating to current religious practice. A recent national investigation established that 49% of Catholics judged that they had to follow the norms laid down by ecclesiastical regulation, while 51% thought that it depended on circumstances or was not necessary.[2] Other research has shown that, particularly in an urban environment, a good number

[1] *Parochies in Nederland op 1 Januari 1966*, quoted above.
[2] *Margriet* (1966), n. 42.

of Catholics thought it not necessary to accept unquestioningly the articles of the faith as prescribed by the Church.[1]

There are more figures available for the decline in the observance of religious practices.

A few decades ago it was usual to go to Mass on Sunday morning and to benediction in the evening. Many went to Mass during the week and to benediction on Saturday. There were also a large number of solemn occasions which drew people to the Church. Then there were numerous religious practices that were honoured, such as the saying of the rosary, morning and evening prayers, novenas, the use of holy water, the veneration of images. The laws for fasting and abstinence were strictly observed. There were associations for prayer and fraternities with a large membership. During the last twenty, particularly the last ten, years many of these practices have been abandoned. Religious symbols disappeared from many homes or were thinned out. Church-going declined, first the benediction attendance, then that of the weekly Mass; the first Friday devotion declined; Sunday benediction was abolished for lack of demand, and the Sunday Mass, too, saw a decline. Many youngsters thought that their parents were 'stricter', more loyal in the practice of their duties and on the whole 'better Catholics' than they themselves.

For a number of towns actual figures of attendance at the Sunday Mass are known. It appears that in the large towns of over 500,000 inhabitants, such as Amsterdam and Rotterdam, there was a noticeable decline from about 50% in 1950 to 35% in 1966. In medium-sized towns of between 50,000 and 100,000 inhabitants the same fact could be observed, while in general the decline was less where there was a higher figure for the Sunday Mass. The situation in the countryside is not known on this point.

Another factor which shows a decline in ecclesiastical practice is the number of communions. In 1955 Catholics aged seven years and older received communion, on an average, 33 times per year. In 1959 it was still 32, but after that it fell to 25 in 1964. That year the rules for fasting before communion were relaxed with immediately visible results the next year when the figure rose to 29.

[1] J. J. Poeisz, *op. cit.*

D

Another factor which illustrates the attitude towards traditional practice is birth control. The Church's regulations concerning this matter occupied an important place in ecclesiastical discipline. But a recent national investigation showed that 73% were against compulsory rules on this point while 84% thought that the Church should either accept the pill or remain neutral in the matter.[1]

The decline in church-going and church practices is easily interpreted as a decline in the life of the Church and religion, and as half-heartedness. And this conclusion is justified if we take the past as our criterion. But it only applies if we speak of a specific form of religious practice, namely that which is identified with the loyal fulfilment of ecclesiastical rules and regulations, in other words, with the kind of religious attitude which prevailed during the emancipation period. Those who still live in that mentality will no doubt judge the others, who can no longer accept that attitude, in these terms. It is a pity that so little research has been done on the nature of the religious attitudes which are developing at present. I have already indicated some of the new features: personal responsibility, acting according to one's own conscience and in ways of one's own choice. Here a genuine social-moral attitude is experienced, just as religious as the strict adherence to doctrine and to liturgical celebration. In the life of the Church this other orientation of the modern faithful is coming increasingly to the fore and leading to a whole range of new applications. Complete adaptation to the new forms of religious practice will only come about when the traditional image of the 'dutiful' Catholic, the 'ecclesiastical' faithful, has faded away.

The organizational structures of the Church

No aspect of Dutch Catholicism attracts so much attention as the organization of pastoral care. In fact, priests and laity are questioning the whole structure. This involves several other issues: the place of the religious orders, training, ecclesiastical management and equipment, financial problems. This discussion is not limited to the spoken or written word. In every field pastoral experiments are taking place which have the important

[1] *Margriet* (1966), n. 42.

function of trying out new ways and means with more or less freedom.

I shall treat of a number of aspects connected with this type of renewal but I will concentrate mainly on territorial pastoral care and the vocational priesthood.

1. *The territorial organization of pastoral care.* The parish, understood in the traditional sense, may perhaps be called the place where the faithful observance of ecclesiastical regulations was most directly 'controlled' or promoted. The parish was both the means and the expression of the solidarity of the Catholic group. Within the parish ecclesiastical authority was embodied in the parish priest, and somewhat less in the curate. This set-up was basic. Every parish showed this pattern in its own autonomous way. Every parish constituted a centre where the submissive loyalty of the faithful found expression in the differentiated social life of the group. The parish was 'successful' according to the intensity of the group's life.

The modern parish is given a very different function. It remains a centre for the most direct approach to the faithful. But the emphasis has shifted in pastoral care from the formation and the life of the group to an individual and pastoral 'moving together' with the faithful. The life of the group which was once the aim of the parish is now becoming the means by which the conscience of the faithful is formed. The *life* of the group has become the *work* of the group, as illustrated by the discussion groups.[1]

The important and central place of the parish in pastoral care explains why a large part of the renewal process is particularly concerned with this problem of the parish. Of all the priests who, in 1965, were active in pastoral care—a total of 4,500—about 82.5% were directly engaged in parochial work and the rest in more specialized forms of work (the forces, industry, youth, education, etc.). They worked in 1,800 parishes and chaplaincies. The renewal process does not concentrate on any single aspect of

[1] Cf. for instance, O. Schreuder, 'De parochie in discussie', in *De nieuwe mens* (April-May, 1965); W.M.I. v.d.Ende, 'Veranderingen in de stedelijke parochie', in *Sociale Wetenschappen* (1963), vol. I.

the parish but touches it at almost every level. It affects the attitude of the priest towards the faithful, the talents of the priest,
the contribution of the faithful to matters of government, the
relations between parishes, the material aspects of the church (the
building), the administration of income and expenses.

There are various plans and projects which aim at reorganizing
the territorial organization of pastoral care. Here priority is given
to co-operation between the parishes, specialization in pastoral
care and democratization of organization and administration.[1]

The tendency to bring about closer co-operation between the
parishes is most perceptible in urbanized communities. The
former system of autonomous parochial units working indepen-
dently of each other has been found inadequate to secure
effective pastoral care in the big town. The emphasis which is
now put on the personal responsibility of the faithful and on the
formation of the individual conscience creates a variety of problems which can no longer be solved by individual priests of one
parish but demand the commitment of a team of priests, with
various abilities. The present parochial structure, however, does
not allow for this specialization. Co-operation between existing
parishes is seen as at least one answer to this problem. Another
answer is provided by so-called pastoral experiments. And here
there are two tendencies.

The first is towards a radical extension of the parish.[2] A large
district of, for instance, 40,000 Catholics thus becomes one single
parish. Within this district there are various opportunities for
services and other activities spread over the whole area. The
whole administration is centralized, and a specialized staff of fifteen to twenty priests is made available for the district.

The second line of experiment aims at a radical contraction of
the parish. Parishes are reduced to a size small enough to make a
genuine communal life possible. This tendency is not so much an
answer to the need for co-operation and specialization as an
attempt to make good the loss of that solidarity and unity within
each parish which existed in the past, and it tries to do so by

[1] *Zielzorgexperimenten; uitgangspunten en opzet* (The Hague, 1965). Report
n. 304 of the Kath. Soc.–Kerk. Inst.
[2] Cf. Schreuder, *art. cit.*

radically cutting down the number of faithful in order to give new life to the group. This overlooks the fact that the faithful no longer feel that their religious life must find expression first of all within the parish group.

Various factors are driving the movement for renewal towards extension of the pastoral units rather than contraction. Important among these factors are the decline in church-going, the expected fall in the number of available priests and the relatively inadequate increase in financial resources. These facts impose a more sober approach to equipment and to working on a larger scale. Thus, to make a church building a working proposition, increasingly larger groups of faithful must be brought together under one parish.

The relation of the parish to the higher level of Church administration is also widely discussed. There is now a general tendency towards a more democratic government and a wider measure of delegation of powers to the 'lower' ranks. At parish level the faithful want to have a voice in parochial matters, while priests are asking for more collegiality in the presbyteries. There is also a demand to reduce the distance between the lower and the higher structures by, for instance, giving the deanery a measure of government and giving it a say in the overall system of appointments. In general there is a demand for more recognition of each one's personal responsibility as opposed to earlier practice when each one was subject to the group and to the ecclesiastical apparatus. For the top level this democratization of the apparatus means a much heavier task. This is being met in practice by extending the diocesan staff with functionaries set apart for specific tasks within the overall administration.

2. *Priests and religious.* Dutch Catholicism faces, rather painfully, a transition from an emancipation type of life to a new type, characterized by the features of an industrial and urban society. During the emancipation period the high degree of solidarity led to a large number of vocations. There was a constant flow of new vocations in the dioceses, the religious orders and congregations, male and female. All indulged in an extensive organization both for training and the exercise of numerous ecclesiastical and social

activities. When the emancipation period came to an end there was a decline in this flow of new vocations, pronounced in the case of Brothers and Sisters, less so in the case of priests. During the first years after the second world war the number of vocations remained more or less constant. In 1953, 46 per 1000 boys of 12-13 entered a minor seminary. From then on the number went down and this decline continues. In 1966, the figure was less than 20 per 1000. This downward trend has accelerated since 1960 and is expected to continue to about half the number of 1966. Figures are being prepared which show the same trend in vocations to the Brothers and Sisters. It is impossible to deal here in detail with the causes of this development, but I wish to point to the far-reaching consequences for training and religious activities.[1]

The serious decline in applications for the *minor* seminary has raised the question whether its continuation is justified. Traditionally these minor seminaries were a special type of school totally aimed at training for the priesthood, with their own educational programme and a type of formation which differed from other schools. This special character has since disappeared. In 1958 there were in Holland forty-two minor seminaries with practically no state subsidy. In 1963 the situation was reversed. Of the thirty-three that still functioned, most were subsidized by the authorities. But this meant that the educational programme had to conform to the ordinary secondary education and could no longer pursue its own line. The specific formation undertaken in the minor seminaries became an equally doubtful matter, at least for practical purposes. Almost 80% of the boys abandon the vocational training, and the schools are frequented by a large number of non-vocational students alongside students for the priesthood. In 1965 there were 1000 such ordinary students and 5000 seminarians proper. One may wonder whether the minor seminaries have not to a large extent lost their function as a specific type of school.

A noticeable reduction in the number of minor seminarians is

---

[1] *Statistiek van de klein- en grootseminaries* (Various years), memoranda of the Kath. Soc.–Kerk. Inst.; O. Schreuder, 'Le caractère professionel du sacerdoce', in *Social Compass* (1965), 1–2; J. J. Poeisz, 'Déterminants sociaux des inscriptions dans les séminaires', in *Social Compass* (1963), 6.

expected. It is estimated that in the 1970s the number will have gone down from 5000 to 2000. Many seminaries are then in danger of losing their claim to subsidies. Moreover, the requirements of training for the priesthood demand larger educational units.[1] This will mean in the long run that of the forty minor seminaries dating from before 1960 only three will remain, if, of course, the need to have specific schools is considered important. In this light it is understandable that there is a tendency to abolish specific seminaries and to use the opportunities offered by ordinary secondary education.

The *major* seminaries felt the new problems later than the minor ones. The suggested solutions have from the beginning been based on the changing situation in Church and society. The educational programme was to take more account of the conditions demanded by a more modern approach to pastoral work. Thus plenty of room has been made for the social sciences. Need was also felt for a more purposeful and efficient organization of the training. In 1965 there were a total of 1,800 students spread over forty training establishments, which means forty-five students per institution. Every institution had its own staff of priests-in-charge, altogether 450. So every ten students occupied about three priests.[2] Greater efficiency was looked for in the concentration of several institutions into a few large ones, with an expert staff and a more varied educational programme. This concentration would also lead to a better fitting in with the universities and colleges. This process of concentration got off the ground rather quickly in Holland. There are such 'concentrated' institutions at the moment in Tilburg, Eindhoven and Nijmegen.

The decline in the number of students for the priesthood will influence the whole question of appointments in the next decade. In the coming years there will be constantly less priests, Brothers and Sisters available to man the pastoral structures that developed during the emancipation period. The age level of the clergy is

[1] *Pastorale beleidslijnen voor de ambtsvervalling van de priester in Nederland* (Publ. by the Pastoraal Instituut van de Nederlandse Kerk-provincie, 1967).

[2] *Statistiek van de klein- en grootseminaries.* Academic year 1965–6 (The Hague, 1966). Mem. n. 163 of the Kath. Soc.–Kerk. Inst.

known to be already high. Forecasts made for several dioceses indicate that the number of parishes will increase while the number of priests available for parish work will diminish.[1]

This demands a reassessment of the nature of the functions to which priests, Brothers or Sisters are appointed. During recent years a number of monasteries have already been closed down. This decline in numbers does not necessarily mean, however, that there is danger for the general practice of pastoral care.

The great number of vocations during the emancipation period led to a vast and wasteful splintering of resources. One has but to think of the forty orders and congregations over which the 10,000 regular priests are divided; then there are ninety congregations of women religious with their 30,000 members and the sixteen congregations of Brothers with 4,100. Each of these orders and congregations has its own complete administration, its own training. In this field co-operation was until recently unheard of. The growing tendency towards integration might lead to a considerable economy of forces. Then, it would be worth finding out how the changed nature of parochial pastoral care might lead to a reduction in the number of priests involved in it. It is not certain that present parish work demands as much work as was formerly the case.

These priests, Brothers and Sisters do not constitute a problem simply because the present structures for pastoral care rest on them. Far more urgent is the problem of the religious as a person and as a human being. As such he enjoys the doubtful honour of standing in the limelight of the present Pastoral Council. Outwardly, the central problem is celibacy, which public opinion no longer sees as a necessary condition of the priesthood, and on the increasing numbers of those that leave. In 1966 sixty priests abandoned their function, a figure which assumes importance when compared with the three hundred ordinations in the same year. The question of celibacy and of leaving is symptomatic of a wider problem which touches the very existence of the priest and the religious. Perhaps it can be compared with the development through which the faithful are passing in their transition from a religious practice based on duty and loyalty to

[1] These forecasts were prepared by the Kath. Soc.–Kerk. Inst.

one of personal responsibility. Priests and religious are, as persons and in their function, far more involved in the behaviour patterns and structures which the Church has imposed on itself. The transition from group responsibility to personal responsibility is for them a much harsher and more laborious process than for the ordinary faithful, and subject to far greater tensions.[1] This is the reason why high priority is given to the priest and religious within the whole field of problems which Dutch Catholicism is facing at present.

[1] Cf. *Over de Priester. Essays en interviews* (Utrecht, 1965; Amboboeken).

6. THE EXPERIMENT

Alfred van der Weyer, o.f.m.cap.

Experimentation is an essential element in the renewal of the Dutch Church. Most Dutch Catholics realize that new forms will not grow out of the old ones just by themselves, but that they have to be discovered by constant experimentation. Standing at the frontier of the promised land the people of God choose from among themselves scouts who must cross the Jordan in order to see what kind of life there lies behind that frontier—what possibilities and what opportunities it offers.

The need for this is particularly urgent since the Dutch Church, perhaps more than other parts of the world Church, has been brought up short before a totally new phase in its history. Until recently caught in traditional structures and defending these structures almost scrupulously, it has suddenly been awakened by the call of Pope John and with a broad gesture opened its doors to all that is going on in the world and so also to the revolutionary developments that are taking place there. From being more Roman than the pope it is now in the vanguard of the renewal. This has brought with it the collapse of the establishment, perhaps with more publicity than elsewhere, and hence the need to find new structures by experiment.

Before we deal with any specific experiments, however, the idea of 'experiment' needs explaining. Not every groping for new forms can be called an experiment, which is a matter of basic modifications in the structure of the Church, not of merely accidental changes. Such changes have always been going on and belong to the normal development of life in the Church. Also, an experiment must be handled methodically; it must start with a definite aim and be carefully planned. Messing about and sensational stunts are hardly experiments. Next, the experiment must be tested from time to time for its viability, it must be submitted to the criticism of the community and be adjusted to whatever conclusions may thus be reached. Finally, ways must be found to see how the experiment, once tested, can spread its influence over the whole community.

In Holland preference is given to the experiment that grows up from below while authority limits itself to sympathetic interest and watches discreetly to keep it within the bounds of the tolerable. But there is also room for experiments from on high, where authority itself chooses certain groups to conduct an experiment and gives them fairly clear instructions how to proceed.

The community of the Church recognizes these experiments because it realizes that the necessary renewal must be brought about along two main lines. The group at large proceeds gradually, and this ensures continuity with the past. The *avant-garde* concentrates on the experiment and risks a leap ahead into the future. Both these lines must run together and will achieve the renewal on condition that the *avant-garde* remains aware of the need to keep in touch with the group at large, and that the larger group shows an encouraging attitude towards those who are trying to forge ahead.

Dutch Catholics are aware of the possibility of failure: that is in the nature of an experiment. But when this happens it should not be rejected as a purely negative result: the community then knows at least that the method used does not lead to the desired end, and the community is that much the wiser. This may well lead to better chances for a new experiment.

In what follows I cannot sum up all the experiments that have been tried out in Holland. I have therefore chosen a few examples that have attracted wide and, in my opinion, justified attention.

The liturgical experiment

The liturgical renewal in Holland is passing through an experimental phase, and shows two lines of development which differ from one another considerably in theory but in practice overlap rather frequently. There is, first of all, the experiment in the full sense of the term, the deliberate attempt, with the knowledge and under the guidance of the hierarchy, to discover the most suitable form for the liturgy of tomorrow by trying out various forms in a tentative fashion. There has also been the pastoral concern to adapt the ritual to the concrete circumstances of persons, place and time. The liturgical development in Holland lies mainly in this pastoral field, though here and there attempts are made that are more strictly liturgical. Since this short essay makes it impossible to draw careful distinctions between the two aspects, I will deal with both under the one heading of 'liturgical experiment', while I would like it to be clearly understood that I take 'experiment' here in the broad sense.

The gradual transition from pastoral adaptation to genuine experiment becomes clear when we look at the three stages through which the liturgical renewal passes. The first stage is that wherever in the world the Roman liturgy is celebrated people begin with an almost literal translation of this liturgy. The second stage is then usually that one sees, more clearly than in the past, what a distance there is between the Roman liturgy and religious practice in one's own country and one's own age, and consequently the need for adaptation is keenly felt. Then comes the stage of real experiment where one no longer starts from pre-existing forms but simply tries to discover, within a broad framework (and tentatively), new forms for the celebration of the liturgy, which are suitable for the Church of tomorrow. These stages do not succeed each other chronologically but one stage frequently begins long before the other is finished. Thus the development may take place in all three stages simultaneously.

The basis for the experiment (in the broad sense) was laid down by the Lenten pastoral letter of 1964. This proposed as the ideal a liturgy which fitted in with ordinary life and which made use of signs and symbols that clearly conveyed the union of all mankind in Christ and through Christ in God. The pastoral letter appeals to all members of the community to help in the creation of such a liturgy:

'We wholly agree with those who maintain that it depends on all of us, that is, the bishops and their helpers, the laity and the religious, whether we can create a really relevant liturgy. We hope that you will think with us, particularly those who are endowed with gifts in whatever branch of the arts, so that we may rediscover a renewed liturgy that is true to life.'

When this letter was published Holland already had several centres for liturgical experiment. They had no mandate, sometimes balanced on the brink of disobedience, met with a rather secret enthusiasm as well as with criticism and were sometimes accused of heresies. The letter gave them new courage. The Commission for the Liturgy, set up by the hierarchy, made official contact with them and reported on their work to the bishops. The hierarchy expressed appreciation of their work in a statement published on 5 May 1956, particularly with regard to the work of the working group for a vernacular liturgy, the *Pleingroup* of The Hague, the 'convent' of secondary schools at The Hague, and the youth Mass of Maastricht. They announced the establishment of a centre for liturgical renewal with the function of investigating how the work already done could be co-ordinated, deepened and made useful for the whole province.

As I cannot enter into all the details of all the liturgical experiments I will simply trace the main lines that run through all the experiments, especially those connected with the Eucharist.

One of the first things one notices is the cutting out of all that is not essential in order to lay bare the basic structure of the liturgical happening. A number of gestures and prayers that have obscured the originally simple character of the celebration in the course of the centuries have simply been dropped—e.g. the prayers at the foot of the altar, the prayers that accompany the preparation of the gifts for the offertory, the washing of hands with its psalm, the prayers at the time of communion, etc. Thus there remains a clean and clear whole which maintains its vital tension from beginning to end.

Within this restored whole there arises, almost spontaneously, a new way of praying. Those who frame the new prayers start from the need to address God in their own language and so express a changed awareness of faith. The following elements are typical of these prayers in the new style:

It is no longer the transcendent God, but the Father who is close to us in Christ; no longer God appearing in his glory but the hidden God of the gospel who cannot be named; no longer

the sacral objective relationship with God, but the human love
in which we commune with the man Jesus Christ; the Church
in her sacramental objectivity is no longer the place where God
primarily manifests himself, but the Church as the locally
gathered community, aware of being one with mankind as a
whole and realizing itself in the sacraments, in God and the
faith.

As an example I quote the concluding prayer which the Amsterdam group uses on the third Sunday of Advent:

'Lord God, Father almighty, you have given us your son as an
unknown man; thus he stands among us, having become the
least of men. We beg of you that we may recognize him
in all the people around us, particularly in those who are
without power and without prestige. In this communion of the
Holy Spirit he lives with you today and every day for all
eternity.'

The experiment obviously did not stop short of the central part
of the Eucharist, the great 'thanksgiving'. In the many varying
Dutch texts that are now current we can discern roughly four
groups. First of all there are the texts that follow the Roman
forms closely, though simplifying it and revising it on a few
points. Secondly, the texts inspired by the older Roman forms,
the liturgy of Hippolytus, the Gallican and the Mozarabic
traditions. And finally those that are based on the present
awareness of the faith. Some of these texts have become widely
known, particularly since they have been incorporated in the
booklets which the faithful use at the Sunday Mass in the
parishes. They have also found much use outside the groups who
take part in the experiment.

The response to the pastoral letter mentioned above has also
led to other ways of renewing the celebration of the Eucharist.
Poets and musicians are trying to develop a new way of singing in
the Church, often using the rich tradition of the Reformed
Churches, and sometimes inspired by negro spirituals, jazz and
beat music. Although not all that is called a 'beat-Mass' deserves
this qualification, there are celebrations which *do* merit this name.
Music is provided by a genuine beat-band complete with guitars
and drums. Occasionally these celebrations are of an extraordin-

arily high standard, sometimes they remain stuck in a pitiable amateurism.

Special mention must be made of what is called the domestic liturgy. It is no longer exceptional that on special occasions (e.g. when there is a discussion evening or a family occasion) the liturgy is celebrated at home, round the table. The priest does not dress in the traditional vestments, but simply wears a stole over his civilian suit. The celebration is adjusted to the concrete situation, the participants are given some part to play, as reader or prayer leader or something similar. Communion is given under both kinds and usually the priest puts the consecrated host into the hand of the recipient.

Much experimenting goes on also outside the celebration of the Eucharist. In many parishes the traditional administration of the sacrament of penance is gradually being replaced by a communal celebration of this sacrament. It is not yet clear how far this way of administering is sacramental. Then, many monasteries are involved in the organization of new ways of celebrating the divine office. A special commission has been set up to co-ordinate their work, composed mainly of members of male or female religious institutions.

All this has led to a high degree of pluriformity in liturgical celebrations in Holland. This obviously has its difficulties and its opportunities. One result is that, particularly in urban centres, the faithful themselves make a choice of the many variations available within certain limits, according to their taste and preference. This breaks down the barriers between the parishes and gives rise to new forms of communal life in the Church, no longer based on the place where people live but on a common attitude to the liturgy.

The ecumenical experiment

The fact that in Holland the Catholic Church is surrounded by other Churches seems to have predestined it to become a kind of ecumenical testing station, particularly suitable for the trying out of ecumenical experiments. Formerly a closed fortress, it opened its gates after the second world war, first gradually, then with broad generosity. In the atmosphere thus created people became aware of an underlying unity between the various denominations, the implications of which demand to be investigated, however tentatively.

Among many others, two experiments deserve particular attention. The first is the attempt to bring about a common celebration of the Eucharist among separated Christians, the search for the possibilities of intercommunion. This intercommunion should be clearly distinguished from 'open communion' where the Church opens its own eucharistic celebration to members of other communions who ask to be allowed to share. Real intercommunion is the meeting of two Churches that recognize each other's Eucharist as an authentic application of Christ's charge 'to do this in memory of me'.

Since the Christmas (1966) issue of *Paris Match,* international attention has been focused on the so-called 'ecumenical Eucharist celebrations' of the Sjaloom group. This gave rise to a certain misunderstanding, in Holland and abroad. Some took it that these celebrations were a kind of ordinary *'agape'*, such as has been going on in Holland for some time. This opinion appeared to be mistaken. The Sjaloom group stated frankly that its celebrations were meant to be genuine eucharistic celebrations. Every Friday evening some Catholics and Protestants meet in the Sjaloom centre of Odijk in order to break the bread together and to participate in the chalice as a commemoration of Christ's last supper.

This same line was pursued at the celebration which took place at the end of the Young People's Ecumenical Congress on 25 February 1967, where some two thousand young people of all denominations discussed their responsibility for the weal and the woe of this world. At a service led by ministers of various Churches the words of consecration were pronounced over the bread and the wine, after which very many received communion.

It must be firmly stated that these experiments did not carry the explicit approval of the hierarchy. In a letter of 15 March 1965 they had approved the *agape* celebrations but stated explicitly that these could not be interpreted as eucharistic celebrations and that, consequently, it was advisable 'not to use wine' with the bread that is the normal food in Holland, 'and in

any case to avoid the separate presentation of these two elements
(of bread and wine)'. In their pastoral letter of 15 February 1966,
the bishops ask, while showing every understanding of the
impatience of the young, that Catholics should stick to the official
attitude of the Church. 'As long as the Churches cannot yet,
however regrettably, accept intercommunion, the members of
these Churches should not do things that contradict the official
conviction of the respective Churches.' The reason for this rejection can be briefly put as follows: the Eucharist is the sacrament of unity and as long as this unity does not yet exist it cannot
be celebrated in common. The reasons behind this type of celebration, however, may be said to be the following.

The presence of the Lord under the signs of bread and wine is
no longer a subject of controversy that has to keep divided
Christians apart and prevent them from celebrating the Eucharist
together. The differences which still exist are predominantly of a
theological nature, and do not affect the underlying common
belief.

More serious are the differences of opinion in the matter of the
ministry. The Protestant minister does not have the ordination
which determines the function of the Catholic priest. But he is
established in his function by the believing community. And this
aspect is being taken more and more seriously in Catholic circles.

Those who agree with 'ecumenical eucharistic celebrations'
emphasize the fact that, in spite of all their divisions, Christians
are basically united in the one baptism and the one surrender in
faith to the Lord. They consider that this unity is a sufficient basis
for—at least occasionally—meeting one another at the table of the
Lord.

They also stress that the eucharistic celebration must not be
seen only as the crowning of a unity already achieved but also as a
preparation for whose who want to achieve this unity. They call
the signs of bread and wine a 'ration of strength on the way',
which man must eat in order to have the strength to restore this
unity on the Christian and universally human level.

The hierarchy has taken account of these motives and
considered them sufficiently serious not to condemn this move-

ment explicitly. They have, however, appointed a kind of liaison-officer who has to inform them and bring out a report.

The second important experiment concerns mixed marriages. Those in charge of pastoral care are trying to explore the possibilities created by the changed attitude of the Church in ecumenical matters, at least in principle.

These attempts lie partly within the limits of the prevailing law of the Church. At a mixed marriage the non-Catholic minister is 'inserted' without tampering with the form of marriage as prescribed by canon law by, for instance, allowing him to give the sermon, or to lead in prayer, or even to join in when the questions are put to bride and bridegroom to which they have to give their 'yes'. And here it makes no essential difference whether the ceremony takes place in a Catholic or a non-Catholic Church.

Some experiments, however, go further. Starting from the point that a civil marriage between two baptized persons is already in essence a sacrament; that the Church can only add a blessing to this already constituted marriage (if bride and bridegroom wish it), and that this can be done equally well in principle by the Protestant minister as by the Catholic priest, some priests prefer to let themselves be guided by the preference of the partners. If they wish to have their marriage blessed in the Catholic Church this is done and, if desired, the non-Catholic minister will be allowed to play some part in it. If the partners want to have their marriage blessed in a non-Catholic Church the priest will respect their wish and keep himself ready to play a part there, if they wish it. The full emphasis thus falls on a common pastoral activity where mixed marriages are concerned, a field which is still almost untouched and where there is need for wide experimentation.

A third clearly experimental attempt at exercising in practical matters the unity which, despite divisions, does already exist, is to co-opt non-Catholics on to the Dutch Pastoral Council. The first —provisional—regulations gave them a place, not as observers but as full members, in the fifteen commissions which constitute the top-level organization of the council. They were also given a seat in the conciliar assembly. This regulation has been modified and this top-level organization has been replaced by an elected delegation of all the faithful, and so the non-Catholic participants have suffered a diminution of their function. It is typical of the experimental situation in which we find ourselves that, when questioned, the organizers of the Council had to admit that they had overlooked this aspect when they reorganized the composition of the Council. It is, however, equally typical that they promised at once to have another look at this matter.

The catechetical experiment

For a long time the Dutch have felt that the present age demanded a new approach to catechetics. This became clear first of all in the religious instruction given in primary schools. As early as 1956 the hierarchy charged the higher catechetical institute of Nijmegen with a complete revision of the 1949 catechism. Immediately a commission set to work on it. They failed to solve the difficulties. Their only conclusion was that they seriously doubted the point of a catechism for children.

As a result the hierarchy dropped the existing catechism at the beginning of the academic year, 1964/5. At the same time there appeared the 'Outlines for a renewed catechetical teaching in schools' (*Grondlijnen voor een vernieuwde schoolkatechese*) which served as a guide for a new provisional approach to religious instruction in primary schools. The most important feature of this experiment was that the old question-and-answer system was abandoned both on the ground of pedagogics (no mere memory work and no starting with formulae but with a kind of learning that involved the whole person) and on parallel theological grounds (faith is not a matter of learning but of living). This put the faith at the heart of ordinary everyday life, with no separate world for the Church apart from the secular world and no separation of religious from secular education. The initiation of the young became a matter which demanded the close co-operation of home, school and Church.

This brought the parents into the question, and very soon revealed the need for a sound catechism for adults. The Lenten pastoral of 1965 put it as follows: 'Parents will only be able to talk with their children about this (*i.e.*, about what the children have learned at school) when they themselves are fully informed about contemporary religious issues through a catechism suitable for adults.'

Yet the real reason why the Dutch Church was the first to work out a catechism for adults lies deeper. Many experts have held for a long time that a genuine catechism can only be developed for adults. Children and young people are best initiated by sharing, in their own way, in the religious life of the adults. This, for instance, was the point of view of the international congress for catechetics, held in London in 1961. The higher catechetical institute accepted this point of view and informed the Dutch hierarchy about it. That same year the bishops gave instructions to start forthwith on a catechism for adults.

Since there was nothing in the whole Church that could serve as an example this catechism was necessarily experimental in character. In March 1962 a basic project was ready, and submitted to about a hundred and fifty readers. Thus some thousands of criticisms were gathered together, not only from exegetes and theologians but also from ordinary fathers and mothers, parish priests and every kind of professional. With this material from which to work a team of experts produced, after three years of solid work, a book that was published as the new catechism (*De Nieuwe Katechismus*). It became a best-seller as soon as it appeared and sold several hundred thousand copies.

At the presentation ceremony of the book on 4 October 1966 Cardinal Alfrink made it very clear that the bishops vested the new catechism with their authority, if not in every smallest detail. He said:

'In offering this book to the faithful the bishops wish to witness to the general "opening up" that has come about in God's Church, thanks especially to the Second Vatican Council. In the preaching of the faith this opening up means that not everything is contained in the rigid formulae of dogmatic sentences and fixed once and for all. It also means that on subordinate points people have a certain freedom of speech, of

feeling and of thought in expressing or following up a definite
train of thought, and yet remain within the unity of faith of
which the apostle speaks.'
He also emphasized the experimental character of the new
catechism.

The new catechism is a book that invites dialogue. It is not
written in the form of question and answer which suggests that
the author has the monopoly of wisdom and that the reader only
has to take it from him. It tries to give an articulate expression to
the mysteries of the faith, to throw light on them from every side
and to place them in the midst of contemporary life. The authors,
as it were, think aloud. The reader can follow the argument step
by step and is prompted to think along with the authors in a
critical way, so that he works out his own position. Nowhere do
the authors try to make it appear as if the last word has been said.
The team has been aware all along that the mysteries of the faith
cannot be summed up once for all; there is always more to be said
about them. In this connection the Cardinal went on: 'It is not as
if with this book all has been said. On the contrary, I hope it will
be the beginning of a living proclamation more adapted to the
gospel.' Living means developing, a constant adaptation to the
reality. It is therefore already certain that every new edition will
be improved in the light of the reactions to it.

Although the development in theology and the achievements of
the Council have been integrated in this book, it has not become a
theological treatise. The new catechism is a broadly conceived,
biblically and liturgically inspired witness to the faith, in which
modern man can recognize his own experience of the faith. It
clearly aims at the new generation. But it is hoped that many of
the older generation can fall in with this witness. It is for them
particularly that the new catechism is shown to lie wholly in the
perspective of the tradition, even though it brings out many new
aspects of revelation.

Its vast circulation will make this book a stimulus towards
renewal in the Dutch Church, not only through primary
education and preaching but also through radio and television. It
will also exercise its influence abroad: at its publication

translations into French, German, English, Spanish, Italian and Portuguese were already being planned.

Experiments in the training for the priesthood

Training for the priesthood is also passing through an experimental phase. I mean here particularly the more advanced training which traditionally prevailed in a number of seminaries and which has recently been concentrated in a few centralized institutes. Instead of piecemeal distribution there is now a tendency to concentrate and incorporate. Apart from this, an antiquated training system is being increasingly replaced by new methods that are better suited to the demands made on the priest in the present age and likely to be made in the future.

This new development was inaugurated at a meeting in May 1963, in Culemborg, where an outstanding figure in the world of the major seminaries read a paper on the reorganization of the teaching of philosophy and theology in the seminaries. He made a plea for much more co-operation which was not exactly irrelevant since in a small country like Holland there were no less than thirty-two philosophy and thirty theology departments distributed over forty-eight establishments. Every diocese, every order and congregation had at least one, sometimes several. Set up when there was a steady flow of vocations, these establishments ceased to be viable when the trend reversed.

At the meeting, mentioned above, a project was discussed, to be worked out in three stages. First, neighbouring institutes should be combined. This was to be followed by the setting up of central theological faculties linked up with an existing university. Finally, a complete scheme for the training for the priesthood would be worked out.

The first stage was completed in 1966. The greatest over-proliferation of seminaries, with their staff and students, was concentrated in the four towns below the Maas and Rhine: Tilburg, Eindhoven, Kerkode and Venray. In this neighbourhood, the study houses were turned into something like community centres. This meant a more efficient use of available talent and converted the many weak institutions into a few powerful centres.

At the time of writing the second stage is in full swing, namely, the linking up with existing universities. It looks as if by September 1967 four of these links will have been established: one in Nijmegen, joining with the Catholic University, one in Tilburg, joining up with the College of Economics, two in the urban agglomeration of Holland: one linking up with the two universities of Amsterdam and one with the state university of Utrecht. It is hoped that, before long, these training institutes will be recognized and subsidized by the state. A little less advanced is the case of Eindhoven where the aim is to link up with the College of Technology. The same holds for the region of South Limburg where it is hoped to link up with the future university of Maastricht.

After this the third stage will be tackled, *i.e.,* once the academic aspect of the training has been settled, the training institutes will no longer be the responsibility of a bishop or religious superior but of an independent board with national status. The training for the ministry will then become the concern of the whole Dutch province and a matter of common interest. When that happens students will no longer come from diocesan minor seminaries or religious communities but direct from secondary schools. The ministers will then join a diocese or religious community only at the end of their training. These training institutes will also make room for boys and girls who want to study theology without going in for the ministry. This will bring about a radical shift in the student population and make wholly new demands on teaching. Those in charge of these projects arc working fast since they must be operative within a relatively short period.

As I said before, this reorganization is not only concerned with a number of practical measures but also means to assist in the formation of a new type of priest. Some features of this development are beginning to become clear.

A priest, trained in the new way, will no longer be the jack-of-all-trades of the past but a fully qualified man. The society of the future will not have room for the priest who is exclusively 'priest', a kind of 'all-rounder', completely at the mercy of any demand his bishop or religious superior may think of, from parish work or specialized pastoral care to purely administrative work.

The future priest must be specialized, either in some branch of knowledge (to qualify him for some teaching post) or in pastoral service (specialized for work at home or abroad, for liturgy, preaching, ecumenical activities, catechetics, youth work). Whatever task he undertakes he will have to be academically qualified on the same level as other specialists, like doctors or lawyers or technicians. This, it is hoped, will put an end to the cultural under-development of the average priest and to the lack of respect for his calling which is a consequence of it, at least in academic circles.

The priest of the future can no longer live in sacred isolation, in his own little clerical world of diocese or religious community, but must take his place in the world of his contemporaries, open to what is happening there, competent to make his own contribution, together with his fellow-citizens, to that world's unfolding. That is the aim of the new training. The priest will not be living in a rural environment but in an urban one. While he studies he will mix with students of all kinds of dioceses, orders and congregations. He will stand with both feet in the common life at the university with which his training is linked, and will meet there students of every kind of learning and of every possible conviction. From the start he will learn to be 'open' in an 'open' world. From this experience he will come to see what kind of priest he will have to be.

A third aspect of the new image of the priest that is being envisaged is the separation of the priestly 'profession' from the vocational choice. In the past these two aspects were always inseparably intertwined: a young man wanted to become a 'secular priest' or Jesuit priest or a Franciscan priest. In any case, at the early age of twelve he opted for celibacy. In the new training the definitive choice is postponed to a much later date. The process is something like this. After the secondary school, where the youngster usually mixes with others, he is going to study for 'church ministry' just as others study medicine, law or technology. After a few years of basic training he specializes for either an academic or pastoral career. The decision to get ordained for the diaconate and priesthood can be postponed till the end of his studies, when he is about thirty. The same holds for the decision to join some religious order. The training leaves room for those who would like to share in the ministry but as married persons. The question, how far such a choice can be combined with the subdiaconate, diaconate or priesthood can be left open for the time being.

In this connection I want to mention briefly the discussion about celibacy which preoccupies Dutch Catholics. The question is whether priesthood and celibacy must remain inseparably united. Somewhat (as yet) amateurish investigations have shown that many have serious doubts on this point. The Church in Holland wants to face this fact and try to bring some clarity into the matter. In their 'Pastoral Directives for the exercise of the ministry in Holland' of 24 January 1967 the bishops said:

'Convinced of the positive value, even for our age, of not marrying for the sake of the kingdom of God, we nevertheless think that the question of whether, for secular priests, celibacy should be optional demands further study and research. We have already taken steps in this direction. And we do this not, in the first place (although we do not exclude it), in order to meet the actual need of individual priests nor in order to cope with a possible lack of priests, but in order to see whether such an option would clarify the new image of the Church and by doing so would bring out more clearly the proper meaning of the priesthood as well as that of the state of virginity.'

The experiment in religious life

A clear example of experimentation is the search for new structures for the life of religious communities. Convinced that it is almost impossible to adjust the situation in established, sometimes centuries-old communities to the present age, there are small groups in numerous orders and congregations that have chosen to experiment to find the best way to achieve a basic *aggiornamento*.

The reflections that guide them have been very clearly expressed by Professor Schillebeeckx:

'The whole concrete set-up of monastic life is in conflict with the real way in which we experience our religion and so deprives the genuine evangelical inspiration of its character as a sign of relevancy and encouragement. Judging by our present factual situation we are living relics of an old culture. And since we share, as living human beings, in the present experience of life, breathe it in with every breath, and often express it even better because we can confront it directly with the tradition in which we still live (in so far as this tradition still corresponds, at least minimally, to the rules and constitutions which are in principle still valid), we all feel the undeniable crisis in monastic life and we are convinced that only major remedies can help; it is no longer a matter of minor changes. For a monastic institution that cannot or will not adapt itself, there is nothing left but to face the consequences and organize its collective funeral."[1]

While appreciating what has already been done in various places, Schillebeeckx is of the opinion that the time has come for a radical reform of the structures. 'Personally,' he says, 'I can only see a solution in officially approved experiments, not outside the order or congregation but within it, and the order or congregation must be generous enough not merely to tolerate this, but to back it enthusiastically.'

For some years a number of such experiments have been tried out. I shall briefly describe one which attracted attention abroad, to give an idea of the kind of thing we are talking about. In Amsterdam three Capuchins, two fathers and one Brother, have gone to live in an upstairs flat, in a popular quarter, like ordinary people. One of them, who used to lecture in theology, works as an unskilled labourer in a metal factory. The other, formerly the brother-gardener in one of the monasteries, works as a gardener in one of the city's parks. The third stays at home to do the housework and to make contact with the neighbourhood, particularly by visiting the sick and the aged. Every morning early they celebrate the Eucharist. In the evening and at week-ends they devote the necessary time to prayer and meditation in which they take their cue from the gospel and then examine the realities of every day in the light of that gospel.

They express their ideal in a small compact formula: 'We want to strive after a life close to the gospel, close to real life as it

[1] *Tijdschrift voor Theologie*, 1967

is today, in the spirit of St Francis and of the Vatican Council.'
Although influenced by the Focolari movement, the French Little
Brothers of Charles de Foucauld and the community of Taizé,
they try nevertheless to give their way of life a Dutch character.

In all this the main preoccupation is for religious life to be
brought into the midst of human reality as it is today. It must no
longer mean 'a withdrawal from the world, an abandoning of the
world in order to find heaven' but it must be among men, striving
with them towards the true humanization of this world and must
make a typical and indispensable contribution to it of its own. This
contribution will consist principally in showing the world, personally and communally, in theory and in practice, that there is a
divine depth to creation, that this creation is borne on divine love
and that it is man's vocation to see to it that this love shall van-
quish. As a special (though not exclusive) Franciscan feature they
add that the poor, in the broadest sense of the word, have the first
claim on this love, according to the saying: 'I was hungry and
you gave me to eat.'

These people see religious life as a bold attempt to achieve with
a few brethren something of that kingdom of God which is
already appearing in this world and is on the point of 'breaking
through'. They do not want to separate themselves from mankind
but to put themselves in the vanguard. They want their simple
existence to be a centre of true evangelical humanism, an
example, a leaven, a call, in a world that is looking for God.

One of the features of this experiment is that it has the full
approval of the ecclesiastical authority, both religious and
diocesan. The provincial and the bishop have given this
full approval because they see in it a possibility to bring new life
to existing and exhausted structures. In the letter in which the
Capuchin provincial announced the experiment, at the beginning
of 1966, he said:

'Since we are convinced of the sincerity of their intentions, we
will not "extinguish the Spirit" but want to leave him all
freedom to do his work in and through them. If we give some
brethren this particular task it is not merely for their own sake
and their own happiness but for the sake of our whole
province. This experiment is approved and commissioned by

the provincial authority. It should therefore not be considered as the personal hobby of a few and still less as a movement that would cut itself off from the province. It is an enterprise undertaken by and for our whole community.'

Those who take part in the experiment are wholly free to shape, within the framework of the three vows and the Franciscan spirit, their whole personal and communal life as seems best to them. Nor are they subject to a time-limit by which they will have to show results. They have been given 'free rein'.

For a year Holland has been alive with similar experiments. Apart from the group just mentioned, there is another group of Capuchins busy at Waalwijk with something similar though slightly different. In Rotterdam there are two Little Brothers of Charles de Foucauld, one of whom is a butcher at an abattoir while the other works as an unskilled labourer in a factory that produces medicines. In Eindhoven, an ex-Trappist is trying with a few others to shape a new life where the morning is given to a secular profession and the afternoon to prayer and meditation. In Utrecht there is a *Koinonia* group with Dominican leanings. In Hazerswoude a few Carmelites have formed a *Diepgang* group, which aims particularly at the young generation. Similar work is being done by the *Pro Mundi Vita* group in Nijmegen.

All these groups have begun to keep in touch with each other and also with Protestant groups with similar aims, such as the *Nicola* group of Utrecht, the *Wingerd* group and the *Spe Gaudentes* group of Amsterdam. The *Nicola* group occupies a key position since it tries to ensure contact among these various endeavours.

What has been said about regular priests also holds for Brothers and Sisters, and lay religious. Here, too, the need is felt for a thorough reform of existing structures, to live in small groups in the world and to follow a secular profession in order to build up a secularized religious life by experiment. All this is very much in the air and one can expect in the coming years a mushroom growth of experiments.

Conclusion

At the start I said that most Dutch Catholics support this

experimentation. But I must add in fairness that this statement rests on guesswork. There has been no scientific inquiry into Catholic opinion at a national level. I also freely admit that this statement remains somewhat vague: there are various ways of 'supporting', enthusiastically, timidly, partially. Hence the following remarks.

It is certain that there is a considerable minority of Dutch Catholics who object to the experiment. They think renewal is necessary but believe that this must come about through modification of existing laws and regulations by the proper authority. One should not try out what has not been approved. Their ideas are strongly 'centralist': they see the renewal as a process that must start from above and be guided from above by the central authority of the Church, that is, Rome. Hence they are highly indignant when somebody celebrates an ecumenical service 'just like that' or says the canon in the vernacular, or tries out a new interpretation of the Eucharist. There is then no argument: this is not possible, it must not be allowed, it must first be approved officially by Rome.

The majority, however, see things differently, although how differently is a matter of conjecture since within this majority there is every shade of opinion. There are some who approve everything, mature or immature, serious or shoddy, well-thought out or purely sensational, as long as it is called 'ecumenical' or 'progressive'. But there are also those who insist that the experiments rest on a vision which can be scientifically vouched for; that it be planned seriously; that the community be given a chance to voice its criticism and that this criticism be heard. I hope to have shown that the experiments outlined above by and large satisfy these demands. They are founded on a coherent theological vision, they are supported by expert institutions, and are accompanied by extensive sociological investigations. It is only because of this that a large section of the Catholic community gives them generous support and that the ecclesiastical authorities make such ample room for them.

These supporters are also divided on the issue of how long these experiments must go on. There are some who see it as a necessary evil, which we should abandon as soon as possible. These people insist on being provided as soon as possible with new anchors, new structures, new religious habits, perhaps even at the Pastoral Council. Others, however, maintain that the experimental stage should run on for some time. They would regret it if, for instance, the Pastoral Council would again imprison the life of the Church in immobile structures and finished patterns. They are prepared to face for a considerable time all the difficulties, the poverty and even the 'de-glamourization' of the experiment, because they think that this is the only way in which a genuine renewal of the Church can be achieved in Holland.

7. THE DUTCH PASTORAL COUNCIL

Henk Suèr

Are Dutch Catholics arrogant? They give the impression that with their Pastoral Council they want to do better than all the bishops of the world at Vatican II. In any case, they have appropriated without batting an eyelid the name 'Council' for an event which bears little resemblance to the Roman spectacle. There is no display of mitred Fathers in Council with their impressive retinue of 'experts', no closed sessions, no solemn proclamations of ecclesiastical decrees.

Let us forget the Vatican example for a moment. Even the Dutch are for once prepared to agree with Cardinal Ottaviani when he says that their deliberations are not a Council in the canonical sense. The enterprise which the Dutch are undertaking does not fit in anywhere with the standard legal pattern of the Church. It has no juridical basis : Canon Law knows of no national councils in which everybody takes part. Although the Dutch are inclined today to consider the code of Canon Law as a mouldering monument, they readily admit that it is more exact to speak of a great 'national pastoral deliberation'. But those that are aware of this lack of connection between the code and the Dutch Council cannot help asking what kind of authority one should attach to the expected pronouncements and decisions. And so people abroad are also fascinated by this experiment because they want to see what this autonomous behaviour is going to end up with.

'We have chosen the name "Council" in order to stress the close connection with the Second Vatican Council,' said the late Gerard de Vet, Bishop of Breda, who started it all. He addressed these words to a gathering of Dutch missionary bishops in Rome before the closure of the Vatican Council. As everywhere else in the Church, the Dutch Church leaders were worried about how to put across the documents and decisions of Vatican II to their own people. For this was the problem with which every bishop returned home. Bishops and theologians agreed that the mere translation and publication of the decrees was inadequate for the purpose, because this, by itself, does not lead very far. To put ideas across one has to mould them into something active. New ideas get stifled when they are forced into old institutions.

It can also hardly be denied that the schemas and decrees of Vatican II are often generalized formulae destined for the universal Church. They are teeming with possible compromises. Their historical background is often alien to existing local situations. Catholic Holland, with its firmly organized Catholic population and its live interest in religious matters, had already initiated a number of reforms.

The Franciscan sociologist Walter Goddijn had already been commissioned by the hierarchy to set up the 'Pastoral Institute for the Dutch Province'. This Institute had already recruited within a few years some hundreds of experts who made extensive studies of important problems. On this basis the hierarchy would be provided with advice. This work covered the most varying matters, from the appointment of press officers for the bishops to the wholesale reform of training for the priesthood. The announcement of the Dutch Pastoral Council came at a moment when from all sides reports and studies began to flow in, and so it was decided to use this material straight away as the first valuable contributions to the coming Council. The quality was, on the whole, of a high standard since the Pastoral Institute had succeeded in enlisting the best experts for their various commissions. It was curious that practically no one who was invited refused, in spite of their own heavy personal work.

One week before Christmas 1965 the bishops, just returned from Rome, had their reports published from every pulpit in the country. The 'dearly beloved faithful' did not understand much of it. Nor, for that matter, did the bishops. But the extensive good-will among clergy and laity made them concerned to take the people along with them in an active search to find out. Was it not said in the then recently proclaimed Constitution on the Church that renewal was a matter which concerned the whole people of God?

The next day there was a meeting of clergy and laity concerned with pastoral care. In a centre for Catholic trade union conferences plans were worked out. The gathering reacted promptly and asked that the deliberations should be based as broadly as possible, so that all could make their contribution on an equal footing. The idea was to involve the whole people in this Council. This was the consequence of the Vatican Council's ideas about collegiality and the responsibility of the laity. The bishops and the representatives of the religious orders and congregations agreed and set up a preparatory commission to continue in this direction. The day after this, Bishop de Vet held a press conference for the Dutch daily and weekly papers, and for radio and television.

'Everyone interested is herewith invited to think with us and to speak up', he declared. This sounded interesting enough. But if anyone asked the Bishop how he thought of making it work he was honestly told that the Bishop was not quite clear about it himself.

The Church leaders however stuck to their guns. Everyone was invited: Jew, Protestant, atheist, sectarian, provo, and, of course, the Catholic. An extra effort was directed to those who were baptized Catholics but had left the Church. One of the earliest moves was to establish a series of postboxes where anyone could mail his ideas, complaints and demands, for the attention of the Council. So far some two thousand letters have come in. They came from villages wanting another parish priest, and from pressure groups wanting to have Latin in the liturgy. Many gave vent to their feelings, the more so as they could remain anonymous. One furious writer exclaimed: 'How is it possible for a priest to behave like a provo?' about a religious priest who had taken part in a protest demonstration against the Salazar régime. Another sighed: 'Would you believe it—I am sometimes jealous of people who go through life without hearing about God?' The Catholic radio began to tackle the public discussion of the material sent in to it as one of the 'postboxes'. Many complained bitterly to the Commission, mainly those who could no longer cope with the pace of the Church's development, and were

E

shocked and feared isolation. Priests then started to correspond with people of this kind.

The material gathered from this 'postbox' campaign showed that one of the most serious problems was caused by remarriage after divorce. This is forbidden by canon law, and if people nevertheless marry before the civilian registrar, the Church considers them as living in concubinage, which for many is intolerable. And so this campaign has led to an apostolate by correspondence and this first rush makes one expect that in the coming years other half-hidden sore spots will be brought home to Church leaders and pastoral clergy. But this does not mean that the original idea behind the campaign has been forgotten, because the content of other letters will be integrated into one or more documents which will be discussed in the Council's assembly.

Another channel through which the Council had already begun to work was the discussion groups. It was obvious that in such a broadly based deliberation the discussion group had to be a vital element. There were already several thousands of these groups, particularly in the diocese of Den Bosch where the late Bishop Bekkers had set up discussion groups in all his parishes. These met, with great enthusiasm, in the evening two to four times per month. Bishop Bekkers was someone who liked to listen just as much as to speak. It is from the reports of these discussion groups that he learned what really bothered the people. There were similar groups in other dioceses, particularly among the students, the clergy and the Protestant pastors. These groups had, in the course of the years, come to replace numerous other Church activities and parochial societies.

The Church leaders soon began to see that the work of the discussion groups was one of the most important elements of the Council. It was already a kind of Council, a rediscovery of an authentic expression of the living Church. This deserved to be encouraged as far as possible in the various dioceses, and the best way of doing this was by distributing varied and clearly formulated subjects for discussion, by stimulating the demand for these discussions from parish to parish, and by seeing to it that the results of these discussions was effectively reported for the attention of the Council via the channel organized by the bishops. Organized in this way several hundred thousand people of all 'thinking' ages are now engaged on relevant discussions about the Church's life in some twenty thousand groups. They keep each other informed and convey to the Council their grievances, desires, demands, ideas, and areas of belief and unbelief. This has opened up a dialogue on a massive scale between the people and the hierarchy. The individual layman can be sure that his voice is heard in 'higher' quarters.

Characteristically, the Dutchman soon began to ask what use all this talking was going to be. It soon became obvious that some method had to be introduced into these discussions to prevent the whole affair from getting drowned in innumerable opinions about innumerable matters. The topics for discussion had been distributed on a diocesan basis, with the result that every diocese was discussing something different. So it became necessary to limit the areas of discussion to those that all could handle. But in order to avoid imposing the opinions of those at the top, who would now be selecting topics for discussion, it was agreed to begin with an impartial sorting out of the subjects which had been sent in, spontaneously, at the outset, and of topics which had already come up in the course of the Council's activities.

It was also clear very early on that the matter sent in, however interesting and enlightening, could never serve as material for a genuine sociological inquiry. As there is an obvious need for such an inquiry, the Catholic Social Ecclesiastical Institute, which had already produced a number of such investigations and could provide the Council with rich documentation, should carry on with its own work. In this it is assisted by the sociology department of the Catholic University of Nijmegen. Important results of these investigations may be expected on Catholic opinion about celibacy and about the state of marriage among Catholics. These and other inquiries are already integrated in the framework of the Council.

The Council was officially inaugurated on Sunday, 27 November 1966. In Utrecht Cardinal Alfrink presided over a solemn liturgical celebration and the Dutch, who like things to be sober, had no reason to complain on this point. Two weeks before the Cardinal had already announced the event with the words: 'In

the Church of today the course of our Pastoral Council cannot be
other than progressive.' He begged the journalists he was address-
ing not to misunderstand him. 'Progressive' did not mean
siding with one or other party, but simply referred to an attitude.
'We are a Church on the move, and in this movement we want to
follow the Lord. He goes on in this world and in this age, and to
follow him means to go forward.' Some find this progress too fast,
he said, others too slow, and this may cause unrest. 'Real unrest,
however, arises from entrenching oneself in one's own opinion,
one's own position. This leads to charges of heresy, and such
charges have always led to the death of love in the Church. Our
Pastoral Council is a free and open exchange in faith and charity,
by which we can break out of our position of entrenchment and
so grow in unity and unanimity.' He added that he had great expectations of the Council though he feared that some might expect too much: 'Every bishop can tell you how he is daily adjured
by extremists to make the most contradictory statements.'

He emphasized the need to think in terms of universal
relationships. This was a chance to serve the universal Church by
making one's own contribution, while accepting that in this service
to the universal Church some limitation is necessary. 'We are not
living on an island: we live and want to live in the universal
community of the Church. Even though we want to have our
own place within this community, we have to take constant care
that we seek and determine this place in relation to and
communion with the whole Church.'

All this was received with murmurs of assent. As reports in the
press showed, the interest of non-Catholics was genuine and
positive. As a national figure Bishop Bekkers had convinced the
average Dutchman on television and in his many contacts with
non-Catholics that Catholics in Holland had a truly modern
approach to religion. This helped to make the Pastoral Council an
enterprise of national interest and to see it as a signal. But many
still grumbled that the whole affair was still far from clear—'it is
all still rather vague'.

The organizers had therefore plenty of problems to cope with.
There was not only the contact with the universal Church, which
was of vital importance, but also the general participation and

constant communication between the leaders and the people.
Goddijn sought the advice of experts in organization and management as to how to approach the problem, which he outlined as
follows:

'The Catholic Church in Holland wants to give guidance that
can lead to a renewal. It wants to do this by prayer, study and
discussion, according to a definite programme, and in stages; it
seeks contact at every level with everybody who is interested. It
has learned through painful experience that such guidance has
no effect if limited to the proclamation of a few new decisions
and ideas. It wants to encourage a renewed life in the Church,
inspired by scripture and the living faith, through a dialogue
with the people. It wants to bear witness to that task which
every man has in this world.'

This consultation led to a particular kind of organization. The
Dutch may well have a bee in their bonnet about organization.
However, they allow sufficient freedom not to stifle the in-
telligence of the improviser, while they remain fastidious enough
to save themselves from sudden embarrassment. The 'paper' concept of the Council deserves some attention because of the unusual and considerable claims it makes.

The structure which the Catholic Church has worked out to
perfection over the centuries is hierarchical: we can picture it as a
pyramidal structure with the broad mass of the least articulate at
the base. Since the inarticulate condition of the faithful layman is
now a thing of the past—and a dialogue between faithful and
hierarchy presupposes in any case a mutual trust and a listening
to each other—the Pastoral Council recognizes that the ordinary
faithful must have a say in these matters. This is only common
sense if the Church is to adapt itself to man's situation and needs
in this modern world.

Walter Goddijn expressed it like this: 'If the Church wants to
put its message across there must not only be mutual goodwill
and openness between the hierarchy and the people, but also
between the Church and those who are of a different faith or do
not believe at all.' This is why other Churches and ideological
groups (Salvation Army, Humanist Society, etc.) were invited to
take part in the Council's deliberation. This invitation also
F

deserved to be accepted since the 'renewal' of the Church was not only concerned with domestic problems but also with those that concern the Church and the world.

The people wanted to choose the direction of democratization, and democracy is almost a dirty word in Catholic ecclesiastical relationships. In any case it is loaded enough to make every theologian scurry off the scene. There was no reason, however, for panic. A commission of outstanding theologians, among them Schillebeeckx, has worked alongside the Council, both in its setting-up period and now it is functioning. These theologians are usually joined by canon lawyers since the Council may lead not only to a new theology of the Church, but to a new Church law. Theologians and canonists have realized that they have to face the question of how far pluriformity can exist within the set-up of the universal Church.

Let us now look at that organization. The bishops of Holland are responsible for the Council. They have entrusted the executive direction to a central commission, presided over by Cardinal Alfrink. He is supported by eleven members, representing roughly the whole of Catholic Holland: bishops, vicars-general, dioceses, religious (male and female) and layfolk (four members, one of them a woman). Two persons from this group are in charge of the day-to-day directions: Monsignor Lambert Rooyackers, sober and experienced, with the confidence of large sectors of the population, and Fr Walter Goddijn, a managerial type who has a sharp mind as well as creative vision. They are aided by an expert secretariat.

So far, therefore, there is nothing out of the ordinary. The hierarchy are still quite safe. With their authority and expertise they peacefully oversee the people, who write letters for the 'postboxes' and continue in discussion groups. Even at this level non-Catholics participate so that the element of the 'other faith' is already integrated there. It was not so very difficult to involve the flourishing Catholic organizations in this event. There was no need to write to each of them: they offered their services spontaneously, and they are really representative of the Catholic scene. These people very soon presented a long list of problems and *desiderata* and suggested topics to be dealt with. They sent in also their reports and documents, the result of their own reflection and their own investigations.

The first meeting, which it had secretly been feared would end in pandemonium, was surprisingly encouraging. It was soon clear that many dozens of societies and organizations shared the same problems—although it was not quite possible to bring pastoral care for the gipsies under the same heading as the re-orientation of the 'Ideas Centre' of the intellectuals! In the same way, the disbanding of specifically Catholic trade unions would have to be handled differently from an investigation into the meaning of 'charity' as administered by charitable enterprises (who, because of the great improvement in official social care, have seen many of their activities superseded).

Most problems came to the fore when the Council's advisers had to be appointed. Originally about forty or fifty experts had been selected impartially enough. From among them a board was chosen to deal with some important matters. This board drafted for the first session a list of fifteen topics which would have to be given priority. It then extended the college of experts to a hundred and thirty-five men and women from all walks of life, experts, people with practical experience, clergy and lay people, chosen either for particular competence in their own field or because they had special influence in publicity, education or various organizations. The choice of advisers was of course closely connected with the list of topics before the Council. Each of the fifteen topics (about which more later) was entrusted to a special advisory committee.

There were some arch-conservatives who had, behind the bishops' back, complained to the Pope about the new catechism which had appeared under the auspices of the hierarchy. There were also some progressive extremists. In a letter to the leaders of the Council a conservative and very learned theologian wrote that the interests of traditional-minded nervous Catholics might suffer through the preponderance of the progressives. The progressives had less to complain about although the students thought that there were too few young people among the advisers (though they exaggerated this).

The leaders of the Council and its advisers met in January 1967 in a slightly festive mood in the brand-new resplendent concert hall De Doelen in Rotterdam. There for the first time a large section of the Council was seen in public. All that went before was but an introduction, and now it was expected that the vagueness surrounding the Council would now disperse. If the day was memorable however, it was for a wholly unforeseen reason: there was a resounding clash between hierarchy and democracy. The college of advisers declared straight away that they were not satisfied with the vaguely formulated measure laid down by the Council's guiding body that the important issue of celibacy and the priesthood should be dropped from the agenda.

The Cardinal finally spoke on the subject: 'The matter has been dropped so as not unduly to delay the treatment of this pressing problem. In the recent past, over a hundred and fifty people have been engaged on preparatory work for a report on the priesthood, and this report will lay down broad directives.'

The audience, somewhat cross, reasoned that if a Council was being held, then the Council should decide such matters. It was replied that, since the work had been done already, it was surely unnecessary to have the work done all over again by a conciliar commission.

Most of the advisers remained suspicious. The matter of priesthood and celibacy had become dynamite in recent years, and it could only rouse suspicion that the agenda had been changed precisely on this point. They had, however, to remain satisfied with the assurance that the bishops would publish their directives within the foreseeable future. In fact, within two months directives came out, and announced among other things that a broad and responsible investigation into the separation of priesthood and celibacy would take place. The Dutch therefore expect something to come out of this at the proper time, though one should remember that an opinion poll does not, without more ado, lead to a change in the regulations.

The advisers had further cause for annoyance, however. They considered themselves at that moment as the representatives of Catholic Holland at the Council. And Catholic Holland would not be satisfied if subjects disappeared from the agenda over everybody's head. What was going to happen to the reports and advice so conscientiously worked on? Could all this be shoved under the table?

During the luncheon recess some advisers hastily drafted a motion in which, roughly speaking, they demanded an assurance that they should decide, together with the leaders, which Council documents would be publicly discussed at the 'plenary assembly'. The majority were in favour and the suggestion was considered.

This point was well taken by the press, as was intended. The next day all the national and many foreign papers came out with: 'Fireworks at the first session' and 'Council Fathers oppose manoeuvre' and 'Clash between leaders and experts'. Perhaps the most accurate headline was that which introduced the report of the famous French Council reporter, Henri Fesquet, in *Le Monde*: 'The Dutch Catholic Church tries to find a new balance'.

The lack of balance between hierarchy and democracy in the organization had become clear, therefore, on the first day. The organization plan had mentioned so-called 'plenary assemblies', public debates on topics before the Council, to be held at least once a session. The plenary assembly could comment in public and propose amendments before the documents would be put to the central commission. This plenary assembly was meant to manifest the country's presence at the Council, allow both majorities and minorities to put their point of view, and thus contribute the formation of a general opinion whilst making clear to the leaders what Catholics were interested in. These assemblies would be open to all the media of publicity. After that the central commission would determine the final shape of the Council documents by a secret vote. The last step would then be (as in Rome) that they would be put to the bishops for confirmation.

For no particular reason many had the idea that this plenary assembly was going to be the same group that met on that day in January in Rotterdam. But was this correct?

The theologians joined the leaders in a study of the still rather inadequate mechanism of the 'mini-Council', as *France-Soir* called it. They reached the conclusion that in the decisive assembly the hierarchy, the clergy, the laity and the religious ought to be represented. All should share in the responsibility, although it ought to be recognized that the bishops had their own irreducible function and the power to confirm or reject the decisions taken by that assembly. It was not difficult to show that the gathering of experts at the first meeting was not a true representation of clergy and people. It did not even adequately represent such an essential group as those directly in charge of pastoral care. In any case, these advisers, chosen from 'above', could not claim any real mandate from the rank-and-file Catholics. Lastly, it is a well-known principle of any organization that a body of advisers is not the executive.

A new statute was mooted. It was again introduced by the Cardinal, assisted by most of the bishops, at a big press conference. The proposed statute was in favour of a supreme body, 'the plenary assembly', which would consist of the bishops and the elected representatives of the Catholic people. How these representatives were to be chosen was still a matter for investigation. This reduced somewhat the statute of the advisory commissions. These commissions, together with the discussion groups, the organizations and societies, and the 'postbox' group, constituted the infra-structure. Each of these sections would create a working group to form together a conciliar board, under the central commission and under the plenary assembly, which would receive the studies, proposals and reports.

Cardinal Alfrink, generally considered an advocate of the hierarchical structure of the Church, declared on this occasion that the Church had:

'. . . its own structure, which, whether we like it or not, is not identical with political democracy and which we cannot twist in this sense. What we can do is to change the present form of this structure which was perhaps too absolutist in a society which now belongs to the past, and to give it a new form. The Church has, by divine institution, a hierarchical structure, and anyone who touches this structure touches the essence of the Church.'

The reception of this statement was mixed, as was already obvious in the discussion at the press conference. Some papers were enthusiastic and declared that the new statute tried to bring more democracy into the Council. Others thought that neither the ordinary faithful nor the bishops were competent to take

important decisions. So what was the meaning of all this talk
about democracy? The hierarchy would not tolerate it in any
case. A third group grumbled impatiently and demanded an end
to all this talk about organization. Could we not make a start with
the real work in good faith?

At the press conference another gap came to light when somebody asked at which point the non-Catholic participants would
come in. One of the theologians present, who had taken part
in the drafting of the new project, disarmingly and charmingly
admitted that the point had been overlooked. This was a blunder,
but it was significant of the trusting mood that prevailed that not
a single non-Catholic wanted to make a case of it. 'We would not
expect, nor would we want, to play a part in the actual direction.
Our role lies more in the field of advice. And we know that we are
granted a full share in that field.' These were the words of
Professor A. Bronkhorst, the official observer for the Reformed
Church, who had also been an observer at Vatican II.

Many Catholics looked out keenly for Bronkhorst's comments
on the new statute in the weekly magazine *Hervormd Nederland*.
He said that he was not surprised at Cardinal Alfrink's opinion
that Christ himself had given the Church the hierarchical
structure. But what is meant by this structure, he asked?

'I myself thought that this referred to the pyramid of
ecclesiastical functions: parish priests, deans, bishops, here
and there metropolitans and patriarchs, cardinals and finally
the pope. It seems to me simply impossible to prove that Christ
can have had in mind such a functional hierarchy. This
prompts some historical observations and it is not only
Reformed exegetes and Church historians who would put in a
few question marks here. However, it seems that what was
meant essentially was that Christ did not want his community
to be without official guidance, and that there should be a certain contrast between official and community. Then one may
readily grant that the forms taken by this official guidance
might vary considerably over the centuries.'

He referred to the general priesthood of all the faithful under
the one High Priest Jesus Christ. The general and local direction
of the Church in the New Testament often had a collegial charac-

ter. After Pentecost Peter and John are often seen setting out
together. The people often played a major part in the choice of
the bishop. He quotes the famous story of Ambrose who became
bishop by popular acclamation. He found it regrettable that in
the course of the centuries the pope more and more frequently
came to appoint the bishop. Such a hierarchy, he thought, had
little to do with Christ.

I have given this quotation because many Catholics in Holland
think on the same lines. And in the same way, many hold that
demands for not only more collegiality but also more democracy
in the Church cannot just be refused by appeal to the hierarchical
structures that have developed in the course of the centuries.
Perhaps the Dutch Council could help here to rediscover an
element of the authentic Church.

The changes and, possibly, improvements in the organization
of the Council will probably take some time, given all the things
that are stirring in this debate. Some people are growing rather
impatient, because all this is not making matters clearer or simpler.
'The supreme Soviet is simple in comparison,' someone remarked
sourly. But it is consoling that in the meantime the Council is
not marking time, although it has not yet much to show. The
advisers' study groups are working on their reports; the thousands
of discussion groups continue to meet and work out their ideas
in the light of their religious convictions; observers, committees
of local organizations, groups of priests and of religious continue
to work out resolutions for the Council, argued and set out in their
reports. It was perhaps worth boring the reader with all these
problems of organization since it has become clear that many
countries and dioceses are closely watching these developments.
There seems to be a desire to use the Dutch experience in order
to do something similar in other dioceses and other countries.

But where will the Pastoral Council ultimately lead? Perhaps
one can start to get some idea when one looks at the fifteen topics
that the first session must deal with:
1. Changes in the Church's life and thought, causes and results;
2. The meaning of a life of faith in a secularized world;
3. Content and practice of religious life for modern man;

4. The moral attitude of the Christian, conscience and responsibility;
5. The liturgy;
6. Putting the faith across to young people and adults;
7. The practice of authority;
8. Sexuality, marriage and the family;
9. The meaning of religious life (monastic life);
10. Ecumenical questions;
11. Questions about strictly 'church' practice;
12. Youth and education;
13. The Christian's responsibility for peace;
14. Church and missions;
15. Work for aid and development.

One may expect that the Council will pronounce on these and other subjects in terms that will appeal to the ordinary faithful as well as to the theologically educated. It will make recommendations to the hierarchy and work out projects for the future. Some, it should be said, think that all this remains too ecclesiastically 'domestic' and that more attention should be paid to the far more serious problems of the whole world. This criticism also implies the argument that the present division among Catholics in Holland will probably disappear when all are fully aware of the divine mission entrusted to everybody and so will accept the commitment to a large-scale attack on need and injustice, discord and illness. Others, however, think that the list of priorities in no way interferes with such a broader commitment. Moreover, there is nothing to prevent a gradual extension of the field beyond the ecclesiastical boundaries if there is unanimity on this point among the majority of the faithful who want to make the Council a success.

One of the most intriguing aspects of this Pastoral Council has been left till the end. One should bear in mind its shaky juridical basis. What is its authority? If the Council is an experiment, is it justified? If later it were to come to the conclusion that the obligation of celibacy should be detached from the priesthood, would one be entitled to proceed on those lines in one's own country? This rather obvious issue has also been put in public to Cardinal Alfrink, who managed to wriggle out of these tricky im-

plications. The answer is more or less known: the margin left to
the bishops or to the episcopal conference for such decisions is not
particularly large. On this point the mini-Council of Holland will
become a colossal test for the development towards more
pluriformity in the at present highly centralized Church. The
tendency towards decentralization is not yet very evident in
Rome. Whatever the outcome of this tug-of-war, one thing is
constantly emphasized in Holland: we are not going to jeopardize
unity with the world-Church. This may demand heavy sacrifices,
as has already been said in various places, and this might mean
that there will be disappointments and that certain things, considered good and justified in Holland, will not come about.

In order to promote this cohesion with the Church at large, an
information service has been set up which sends all the
documents carefully translated into various languages to the
pope, the heads of the departments of the Roman Curia, the
presidents of the episcopal conferences of Europe and other
interested bodies. When necessary direct contact is made with
officials in the administration of the whole Church or with other
authoritative figures in order to keep them informed with what
people in Holland think and want. And in this way it is hoped to
receive stimulating suggestions that can be useful for the
discussion at home and for the living unity of the universal
Church. These contacts are actually in progress. The leaders of the
Dutch Council have, however, announced that when the Roman
administration does not agree with the Council's decisions or
opinions, they will insist on a thorough explanation of its motives,
and this explanation will also be made public in Holland.

Is this to be taken as a threat? We do not know how all this is
going to develop. What is most important is what Schillebeeckx
said in public at a conference in Rome, in all likelihood with the
assent of the Dutch hierarchy. He declared that the decrees of
the Dutch Council should not be put to the various curial
authorities but to the Synod of Bishops, who, together with the
pope, constitute the supreme authority of the Church. 'In this
way important decisions of one province of the Church will be
taken in peace with the Church as a whole.'

8. HOLLAND AND ROME

MGR. DR. JAN C. GROOT

The Roman Catholic Church of Holland has begun to concentrate its energies on thinking about the way in which it can be, in the most lively and fruitful manner, the embodiment of the serving Church of Christ in the midst of its own people, who are developing at an accelerated pace, and with its eyes trained on the whole world where a new society is being created. It wants to do this in the closest possible communion with other Churches that have declared themselves ready to share in this thinking and searching with a genuine warm spontaneity, and also in dialogue with those who have chosen a different philosophy of life. In this the Dutch Church is conscious of its own inalienable responsibility as a local Church to give the universal Church of Christ an aspect that fits in with the situations, desires, issues, sensibilities and possibilities of this country, and which nevertheless fits in also with the unity of the one Church. From the start it has also been concerned with finding a way of setting up its own system for contemporary and conciliar consultations which would make it possible for all the faithful to feel themselves actively involved in the sharing of this responsibility.

This project, launched by the bishops themselves, has been the subject of widespread interest abroad, from the very start. This was, of course, largely due to rumours about a religious and ecclesiastical crisis in Holland that had found wide currency. Most of these rumours were based on experiments that were indeed very original, but were not always truthfully reported nor correctly assessed, so that in this peculiar light the whole Catholic population of Holland was endowed with a certain image that left all distinctions out of account. In several interviews the question was repeatedly put as to how the Pastoral Council stood with regard to the supposed tumult that beset the mind of Dutch

143

Catholics. In a more or less overt way this was then formulated
into leading questions about the possible threat of a schism. The
approach was similar to that of the Italian press at the beginning
of the fourth session of Vatican II.

Others, however, less prejudiced and with a broader understanding of the situation in Holland, saw that this Pastoral
Council linked up with the tendencies towards a renewal of the
Church, as traced in outline by Vatican II and proposed to
bishops and faithful for working out in practice. And this is
obviously the truth of the matter. Thanks to sound information
provided by press, radio and television, the Dutch, who are by
temperament interested in religious matters, were given the
opportunity to follow happenings at Vatican II with a critical eye.
And since the Dutch are inclined to carry thought into action,
theory into practice, words into deeds, they wanted to pass as
soon and as consistently as possible from the much applauded
plans for renewal to their actual realization. They wanted to take
seriously the pluriformity that was recognized in principle, and
this inevitably implied the relative autonomy of local Churches.
They wanted to see religious liberty applied to the increasing
number of mixed marriages. They wanted to draw the practical
conclusions from the new respect for other Christian Churches
and take a new look at the problem of intercommunion. And so it
was this typically Dutch inclination not to be content with
slogans and to turn the proposed renewal of the Church into
actual fact, which interested this second group of interviewers.
These people were aware of the dangers implied in a reforming
Council that remains ineffective and were therefore most
interested in any move that led in the right direction; they did not
remain content with superficial criticisms. And so they saw in
what happened in Holland not merely a danger but a sign of
hope.

It will be obvious that this desire to be the Church of Christ in
a genuine Dutch way is bound to raise problems and tensions
connected with the maintenance of unity with the universal
Church as it is centralized on Rome. But this is not necessarily a
threat of schism. Nor is the problem as such a peculiarly Dutch
problem. It is inherent in any serious consideration of the specific

responsibility of local Churches and local bishops. It is the inevitable result of an emerging pluriformity. It is therefore a healthy problem, of the highest interest for the true catholicity of Christ's Church. Trying to prevent or eliminate this problem out of fear or suspicion simply means that the local Church suffers in its own dignity and is violated in its own responsibility, and this, in turn, means that one no longer really accepts the Christ-willed unity of all local Churches. The reason is that the problem can only be avoided by a simple-minded sacrificing of pluriformity to uniformity or by a one-sided overrating of local autonomy and autocephalous independence at the expense of the necessary unity. The evil of both ways of simplifying the matter is clearly illustrated in the history of both Eastern and Western Christianity.

The full implications of the problem lie embedded in the documents of Vatican II, and this is a credit to the Council. It is to the credit of the Council that it has once again strongly emphasized the importance and irreplaceable significance of the local Churches and the inevitable consequence of pluriformity within the Church after such a long period of one-sided emphasis on overrated centralized unity. Both the Constitutions on the liturgy and on the Church as well as the Decree on the pastoral function of the bishops put forward the local Church as the concrete and actual embodiment of the whole mystery of the Church at a given place and a given time. The local Church is no longer treated as a little piece of the whole Church but as the whole Church itself in its local and temporal presence.

This links up clearly and consciously with the mind of the early Church and of scripture which not only calls every local community of believers a 'Church' but also explicitly speaks of the one Church which is there present in Jerusalem as well as in Corinth, Ephesus, etc. This seems to show quite clearly that the local Church must be seen as a concrete embodiment of the one Church with all the richness of salvation with which this one Church is endowed.

According to Vatican II, then, the local Church is not primarily a subordinate part of a greater whole, a part which has only obediently to fit in with the whole in order to partake of the glory

of the whole. While undoubtedly part of something greater, the
local Church is itself that same total mystery which also lives in
the whole. This is precisely the importance of the local Church.
Only in and through the local Church is the whole Church of
Christ rooted in our earth, a concrete phenomenon of our history;
it is thus that the universal Church will not become a platonic
idea and hover above our human condition. Only in the many
local Churches is the one Church of Christ alive in our midst.
And so it started upon its way through history as a local Church
in Jerusalem in order to be present in the same total way in other
places 'unto the ends of the earth'.

Since all local Churches are concrete embodiments of the one
Church of Christ in the same way, they can, all together, only be
the one Church in its concrete distribution over the earth and
throughout history. All together are the one world Church. In
this world Church—the sum total of all the local Churches—there
lives the same total mystery and the same structure which are to be
found in each of the local Churches. This is why each local
Church also has the care and responsibility for the one Church.
But it bears this responsibility in common with all the other local
Churches. This means that this responsibility must work in the
context of the world Church.

What, however, the individual local Churches do not have but
the world Church does, is the unfolding of the catholicity of the
one Church of Christ. Since all the local Churches are limited
variations of the total Church, the world Church is the organic
unity of all these variations. These, taken together, express the
riches of the mystery better than any individual local Church, and
in their overall unity reflect that dominion of the Church of
Christ which stands open to all people and all cultures.

The local Church shows itself most emphatically as the
concrete embodiment of the whole mystery of the Church,
according to Vatican II, when it is gathered in eucharistic
communion under the presidency of the bishop round the table
of the Lord. It is then consciously gathered round a servant,
entrusted with the fulness of the sacrament of ordination, who
can therefore administer the word and the sacraments in their
fulness within the Church. At that moment and in the

sacramental sign of the bishop's preaching and the bishop's breaking of the bread, the local Church stands in the presence of that one bread of life that gives itself totally to all in order that all may believe and be nourished. That is when the mystery of living communion with Christ takes place, the mystery in which the whole Church lives as it becomes conformed to Christ.

But this mystery of living communion must really penetrate into the awareness and life of the faithful. It cannot be a mystery of life unless it is assimilated. And it can only be assimilated by *real people* who differ widely from each other through environment, climate, temperament, culture, history, the pace of development and inborn sensibilities. The Church therefore only really comes to life by being assimilated in various ways, determined by these differences among the peoples.

Before we see in this pluriformity a danger to the ecclesiastical unity of the Church, we ought first of all (and most of all) to appreciate the fact that this pluriformity is the incontrovertible condition for any concrete life of the Church in us human beings. And then it will appear that a true pluriformity, instead of jeopardizing the unity of the Church, promotes it in many ways because this is the only way that this unity can exist and only in this way can the catholic and apostolic character of this unity be made manifest. The unity of the Church is a unity round one Lord, who wants to gather to himself all peoples with all their gifts and talents and who will not deprive them of anything that is of value. In its apostolic origins this unity of the Church left room for a pluriform expression of the mystery of the Church. One diminishes the apostolic character of this unity by obstructing the various ways of expressing it.

It is because it wanted sincerely to renew the life of the Church and bring about a fuller manifestation of its catholicity and apostolicity that Vatican II made such a powerful plea for pluriformity in the Church. Nor did it wish to limit this pluriformity to a few innocuous variations in the celebration of the liturgy. It wished to extend this pluriformity to the whole of the Church's life, as is clear from what the Decree on ecumenism said about Catholic participation in the ecumenical movement:

'While they safeguard unity in essentials, all in the Church should retain a lawful freedom, corresponding to the gift that each has received, in the various kinds of spiritual life and discipline, in the variety of liturgical rites, and even in the theological development of revealed truth. In all things they must cultivate charity. By this procedure they will make a demonstration, which is daily more complete, of that catholicity which deserves the name, and of the Church's apostolic character' (n.4).

The responsibility for the way in which the one Church will be embodied in a particular locality at a particular period so that it is a truly serving and truly living Church rests obviously in the first instance with that local Church itself, in communion with its local bishops. Only its factual relationship with local developments can help to form a responsible judgement in this matter. For a number of dioceses to be joined in a synod, in order to decide responsibly on the particular form the embodiment of the whole Church must take under local conditions, has always been a spontaneous phenomenon in the life of the Church. Whenever the needs of the time demand it, such a synod should meet. And as the issues that arise begin to extend to other peoples and to a wider context—perhaps even to a whole continent—the synod will have to extend its composition correspondingly. This will then express in a tangible manner the communal responsibility of the local Churches for the communal life of the Church. This synodal structure is concerned with nothing less than the very life of the Church, while giving expression to the cohesion of these dioceses.

This, in any case, was the conviction of Vatican II which, in its Decree on the bishops' pastoral office in the Church, stated:

'From the very first centuries of the Church the bishops who were placed over individual Churches were deeply influenced by the fellowship of fraternal charity and by zeal for the universal mission entrusted to the apostles. And so they pooled their resources and unified their plans for the common good and for that of the individual Churches. Thus there were established synods, provincial councils, and plenary councils in which bishops legislated for various Churches a common

pattern to be followed in teaching the truths of faith and
ordering ecclesiastical discipline. This sacred Ecumenical
Synod earnestly desires that the venerable institution of synods
and councils flourish with new vigour. Thus faith will be
spread and discipline preserved more fittingly in the various
Churches, as the circumstances of the times require' (n.36).

Although there is here a rather one-sided stress on the common
responsibility of the bishops, it is clear from the whole context of
the Decree that there is no intention to exclude the priests,
religious and layfolk from this responsibility. On the contrary,
the bishops are strongly urged to share and promote this
responsibility.

It is, however, curious in the documents of Vatican II that,
alongside this striking appreciation of the particular nature of
the local Church, there appears at times a seemingly exaggerated
stress on the oneness of the world Church as a reality centrally
based on and guided by Rome in common with the bishops of the
world. Fear of personal responsibility in many a Father of the
Council found expression in repeated warnings to remember this
centrally guided unity.

Everyone is of course convinced that this unity should not be
overlooked. For every Catholic the successor of Peter is more
than merely the head of a local Church so that he also has a
function to fulfil with regard to all other local Churches. But it is
equally obvious that this centralization of the world Church has,
in its empirical form throughout the centuries, created a tension with the necessary individuality of the local Churches.
And so Vatican II, which wanted honestly to examine the
empirical reality of the Church critically in the light of the gospel
and was therefore prepared to accept a reform of the Church, has
put before us the extremely serious issue of how far the
distinctive conduct of the local Churches may go without
damaging or even disrupting the necessary unity. In other words,
the question we must answer is this: granted the recognition of
the distinctive character of the local Churches, what must be
preserved in order to remain true to the Christ-willed unity of the
whole?

This issue is still further complicated by the fact that it has

occasionally happened that some things were put forth as
necessary for this unity which on examination were seen to
belong to the province of free decision. When, for instance, we
think of the way in which Latin as a liturgical language was so
often linked up with the unity of the Church and therefore was
said to promote this unity, we can hardly be astonished that
suspicions have been roused that in matters of faith too there
have been glib arguments which cut out the distinction between
what had to be accepted in order to preserve the unity of faith and
what was merely a time-conditioned and therefore one-sided
theological explanation. This suspicion is the more justified since
it is clear that, particularly in the West, so little distinction has
been made between the unity of faith and the unity of theology.
It is therefore extremely difficult to establish accurately what is
and what is not proposed by the Catholic Church as essential to
the unity of faith. Every theological textbook is inclined to give its
own interpretation so that the number of essential dogmas varies
from one textbook to another. This also creates many difficulties
in the dialogue with other Christian Churches. And in so far as
discipline is concerned we have to realize that we have only
recently started to turn our back on the period of complete
uniformity so that we are not yet accustomed to a certain
freedom of movement in matters which are certainly not essential
to unity and can therefore be dealt with on the lines of a certain
pluriformity. It is still too easy to label as 'disloyal' those variations that differ from the hitherto universal pattern in discipline.

Thus there is a whole field of tensions connected with the
particular nature of the local Church and with pluriformity. It is
a field where the precise means of maintaining both the general
unity and the distinctive character of the local Church are still far
from clear to everybody. The local Churches and their pastors
need to be trusted to a high degree if we want to find a sincere
solution to this problem.

The Dutch Church is today fully aware of this problem. And,
of course, it reacts to it in its own peculiar way. How else could it
react? It must be stressed, however, that as a whole it is very
conscious of the fact that, like all other local Churches, it has to

face this issue. Like others, it has to answer the critical question whether and how far each local Church can embody truthfully the one Church of Christ while at the same time doing so in its own local fashion. Every local Church can become unfaithful to its mission. Only the Church as the one living temple of the Spirit, gathered round the one gospel and the one eucharistic table under the presidency of those who have the fulness of the apostolic mission, can be confident that it will be kept together in loyalty to the Bridegroom and so be confirmed as the pillar and foundation of the truth. Only in so far as a local Church is inserted as a living stone into this temple, as it was actually inaugurated in Jerusalem, and therefore does not start to govern in a self-opinionated autonomy outside this temple, can it be sure that it is the true Church of Christ according to Christ's intentions. The Dutch Church has no intention to break this living link with this one living temple.

Nor has the Dutch Church any intention to abdicate, in an irresponsible manner and against the spirit of Vatican II, its proper responsibilities for its own way of being an authentic embodiment of the Church. It has learned to be somewhat critical towards exaggerated unity slogans. After a long period of ultramontanism, imposed by the circumstances of the time, during which it learned all about its commitment to the world Church and expressed this in a powerful missionary spirit, it is now being increasingly occupied with its own problems. Thanks to the movement of emancipation in social life, it has become more and more conscious of its task and significance in its own country. A new and scientifically thought-out reflection on the faith began to shape itself, and here the knowledge of various languages, so indispensable to a country like Holland, enabled Dutch Catholics to listen carefully to the critical questions put by a theology of renewal that was also alive in other countries. Thus the Dutch Church was able to catch up in fields where it had undoubtedly fallen behind.

The post-war problems created by rapid development at every level of society forced it to set to work on its own contribution to the renewal of the Church. This process took place in the context of a dialogue with Christians of other Churches, which became particularly urgent in the years after the last war. Clergy and laity, professional theologians and not so professional ones took part in this. This is why this dialogue broke through the chilly atmosphere of purely academic conversations, and was animated by a genuine spirit of friendship and that 'togetherness' which was born in the war years. Thus the Catholic Church in Holland became familiar at every level with the critical issues, put for centuries by the Reformation to the Church of Rome, but never properly listened to. And in this way Dutch Catholics made the surprising discovery that many of these questions appeared to coincide with those put by Catholic theologians in recent times and voiced even in the sessions of Vatican II.

This brought it about that the new self-awareness which took place in the Dutch Church after the war developed in a definite ecumenical context. The result was a growing sense of belonging together and also a deepening conviction of the importance of the distinction, seen by the Reformers, between the Church in its empirical and outward form and the Church in its purely evangelical form. This distinction was also applied to the Catholic Church as it is gathered round Rome, and not everything found there was seen to be the pure gold of the gospel. Nor could they acclaim and applaud everything the Church had done in its historical development in terms of exclusive and unadulterated progress. This was particularly visible in the way in which the unity of government had developed historically.

When one remembers the dislike of the Dutch for futile and purely academic discussions, one can imagine that there was a certain impatience to get down to work in the highly necessary renewal of the Church and, by the same token, an increasing dissatisfaction with forces constantly obstructing this renewal process from within the central government of the Church. It is surely understandable that not everybody managed all the time to achieve the perfect balance. For, although by no means revolutionary, but rather conservative by nature, many Dutch Catholics became uncertain about the lasting and unchanging values of the faith. This was connected with the powerful re-formulation of many critical questions of the nineteenth century, which were then left without an answer, but had re-emerged in the twentieth.

These questions concerned the connection between humanity and Christianity, revelation and history, life and the many changing forms of life. They queried what should and what should not remain permanent throughout all centuries, what should and what should not be considered as true history in the witness of the Bible. This led to many uncertainties in many people, who were occasionally provided with an irresponsible and premature solution. It was on this kind of thing that attention abroad seems to have concentrated, rather one-sidedly.

With his old, historically developed sense of freedom, a freedom which always found an outlet in Holland in freedom of speech, the Dutchman is not accustomed to mince matters but likes to prompt widespread discussion by saying publicly and plainly what he thinks. Hence, to the displeasure of many in Rome and elsewhere, the Dutch press, radio and television boldly stated whatever criticisms or dissatisfactions had been expressed with regard to a Rome that still possessed the mentality of strongly centralized unity. This was not precisely the best way of gaining the confidence of Roman circles.

It was in any case not easy for Holland to obtain the unlimited confidence of Rome. It had, since the Reformation, the reputation of being a Calvinistic and therefore heretical country. For centuries it was the problem child of Propaganda Fide, a child who, from the ecclesiastical point of view, could not stand on its own two feet. Dutch Catholicism was therefore easily suspected of being more or less influenced by Calvinism, which would not exactly be considered healthy in Roman eyes. The open and frank expression of criticism, impatience and dissatisfaction was therefore bound to bring to life again the suspicions that were still lurking in the background at Rome.

On the other hand, it is only fair to say that, in Rome too, there has been readiness to allow room for the renewal process in Holland. At a time when the suspicion of 'false irenicism' was still freely bandied about, Dutch ecumenical initiatives could count on the goodwill and support of many a member of the Curia whose name would certainly not have been thought of in this connection during Vatican II. It was unfortunately frequently the ultramontane mentality of some Dutch circles that systematically kept Roman suspicions alive.

And so the Dutch Catholics are looking for a new relationship with Rome which maintains a healthy tension between unity and the local Church and where neither is sacrificed for the sake of the other. Non-Catholics show on this point an interest hardly thinkable in earlier days, because the whole of Holland is watching the result of this honest search.

Often we are asked in connection with the Pastoral Council what would happen if Rome should refuse to accept one or other attempt in this effort to be the Church of Christ in a truly Dutch way. Obviously, difficulties are expected, and here one thinks particularly about the possibility of dissociating the priesthood from the law of celibacy in Holland, as in fact already happens in isolated cases. If Holland were honestly convinced that this was a way which would help the life of the Church in Holland, would Holland insist? Could it develop its own ecclesiastical discipline in a matter which, even according to Vatican II, is not essentially linked with the unity of faith? Would it be allowed to? Such a special ecclesiastical discipline in this field could be honestly compatible with a high appreciation of celibacy as a commendable option, as is the case in Eastern Churches. It would not have to conflict with the Church's *sensus fidei*.

I have already given my honest conviction that Catholic Holland is in no way steering towards a schism, in spite of what so much of the press has said. Schism would help nobody. Nor would it help the renewal of the Church in Holland. But the Dutch are likely to make use of the possibilities opened up by Vatican II in view of such a renewal. The Dutch will obstinately cling to this, as is their nature, and they will not lose their heads for the sake of glib slogans. They will also act with the greatest caution, where nothing is held for certain unless it really is so. Their sense of realism will also take account of the fact that not all Roman circles are equally overjoyed with the renewal movement set off by Vatican II.

In all this it is realized that in many ways the path of an antiquated Roman uniformity or flattening centralism will cross the path of the Church's renewal in Holland. The Dutch are level-headed enough to accept this fact without too much excitement. Just as Rome was not built in a day so the renewal of the Church will not come about in a day.

If, however, this is not going to lead to a deadlock, fatal to both sides, a serious dialogue must be set going between the remaining centralizing element and those who want to achieve pluriformity. This must not be a monologue where only the Roman Curia or, if you like, the watchful Congregation of Doctrine is the only voice to be heard. Nor should they be reduced to silence. There must be a constant exchange so that there is a chance of a genuine assessment of values and arguments.

Moreover, this dialogue must take place with the body that is genuinely charged with the government of the world Church. This seems no longer to be, since Vatican II, the pope surrounded by the Roman Curia, but the pope surrounded by the episcopal Synod that assists him in the government of the Church. This is put explicitly in the Decree on the bishops' pastoral office in the Church:

'Since it (the Synod of bishops) will be acting in the name of the entire Catholic episcopate, it will at the same time demonstrate that all the bishops in hierarchical communion share in the responsibility for the universal Church' (n.5).

The text here concerns the pastoral care which the bishop of Rome exercises over the whole Church and in which the episcopal Synod clearly shares. This is why this Synod is seen as 'rendering especially helpful assistance to the supreme pastor of the Church' (*ibid.*).

From this it would seem rather obvious that the Roman Curia, which until recently seemed to be surrounded with an aura of papal authority, has been given a more modest place than was the case in the past. It appears to be there to serve not only the pope, but the pope plus the episcopal Synod, and by the same token, to be subordinate to a more collegial and episcopal government of the Church. And so the question as to where the real power lies in Rome may be determined more clearly in the future.

In any case, all this will lead within the central government of the Church to more room for the so very necessary and fruitful dialogue between unity and pluriformity, between the world Church and the local Churches. For, in the episcopal Synod all the local Churches are represented and therefore by implication share the responsibility both for unity and for pluriformity within the Church.

Hence the tense expectation with which people will watch this Synod. Through the local, national and continental episcopal conferences, so powerfully stimulated by Vatican II, questions can be put on the agenda which deal with the real life of the Church. This real life is, indeed, not an abstract idea of one Church, but the life of the one Church as embodied in the many local Churches, which all have their own individuality in spite of their communal oneness.

NOTES ON CONTRIBUTORS

Jan Groot. Born 1908, studied theology at the seminary of Warmond (diocese Haarlem) and at the Catholic University of Nijmegen. In 1946 he published his thesis, *Karl Barth en het theologische Kernprobleem,* which was followed by a study on *De theologische betekenis van Karl Barth.* Since 1937 he has been a professor at Warmond Seminary. He has been one of the foremost pacemakers for ecumenism in the Dutch Catholic community, and since 1960 president of the Willibrord Vereniging and delegate for the Dutch episcopate in ecumenical affairs. As an official observer he attended the World Council of Churches gatherings at New Delhi and Montreal. During the Second Vatican Council he was one of the advisers of the Dutch bishops and a much sought after *peritus.* He has published widely in magazines, annuals and studies on ecumenical affairs.

Alfred ven de Weyer. Born 1922, studied theology at the seminary of the Capuchin Fathers and political and social sciences at the Catholic University of Louvain, Belgium. His thesis *De religieuse praktyk in een Brabantse industriestad* was widely applauded and got the Henri Velge prize. From 1955 till 1963 he worked as an adviser for the Catholic Labour Movement to sponsor spiritual education and development. Since 1963 he has been a religious journalist, publishing in seven regional Catholic daily newspapers. In this capacity he covered the whole of Vatican II and collaborated in many radio and television programmes on this subject.

Michel van der Plas. Born 1927, covered Vatican II for the news magazine *Elseviers Weekblad* and published a *Dagboek van het Concilie* (2 vols). Together with Bishop Bekkers he wrote *Gods volk onderweg* (U.S.A. edition by Holt, Rinehart and Winston). Besides having published ten volumes of poetry and translations (Shakespeare, Eliot, MacNeice, Fry), he wrote a documentary book on Dutch catholicism between the two world wars (*Uit het Rijke Roomsche Leven*) and recently published with Huub Oosterhuis, a new translation of *50 Psalmen*.

Joseph J. Poeisz. Born 1935 at Leeuwarden; degree in sociology at Groningen University in 1959 (*cum laude*). At present on the Staff of K.S.K.I. (Eccl. centre for research and advice). His activities cover religious sociology, planning for churches and schools, and ecclesiastical statistics. Is secretary to the working-group of sociologists and psychologists of the Dutch Pastoral Council. Published, among other things, articles on vocations for the priesthood in *Social Compass* and on Dutch Catholic practice in *Internationales Jahrbuch für Religionssociologie*.

Henk Suèr. Born 1932 at Amsterdam. After secondary education studied first modern languages, then history and sociology. Since 1954 one of the editors of the daily paper *De Tijd*, now chief news editor. Wrote among other things *Goden van de Engelenbak* (history of the Dutch theatre) and *Het dagelijkse leven in de 19e eeuw* (daily life in the 19th century), both published by *Het Spectrum* in De Meern. Has made many journalistic contributions on social, cultural and ecclesiastical matters, at home as well as abroad. Has now, for some years, concentrated on revolutionary future developments in medicine, biology and automation. Is adviser to the Pastoral Council on the commission on 'Marriage and the Family'.

Nico van Hees. Born 1915, priest-journalist, works since 1 June 1966 as general reporter on the staff of the socialist daily paper *Het Vrije Volk*. Became a Jesuit in 1934, studied philosophy, Dutch and theology, was ordained in 1949, and taught Dutch and religious knowledge at the Jesuit College of St Ignatius in Amsterdam. In 1954 he joined the editorial staff of *De Linie*, and concentrated on journalism, writing about domestic and foreign politics and social matters, such as marriage and birth-control. In 1963 the weekly Jesuit paper *De Linie* became lay-controlled under the name *De Nieuwe Linie*, but his authorities allowed him to continue his activities on that paper. In 1964 the General of the Jesuits objected to the paper's policy and without consulting the lay directors of the paper withdrew all Jesuits from the staff. After having been a Jesuit for thirty-one years van Hees then left the Order on grounds of principle and was accepted as a secular priest in the diocese of 's Hertogenbosch by the late Bishop Bekkers, whose biography he wrote under the title, *Bisschop Bekkers, vriend van ons allen* (Bishop Bekkers, friend of us all).

INDEX

160